Coal
Miner's
Son

David Perkins

WESTBOW
PRESS®
A DIVISION OF THOMAS NELSON
& ZONDERVAN

Scripture taken from the King James Version of the Bible.

WestBow Press books may be ordered through
booksellers or by contacting:

WestBow Press
A Division of Thomas Nelson & Zondervan
1663 Liberty Drive
Bloomington, IN 47403
www.westbowpress.com
1 (866) 928-1240

ISBN: 978-1-5127-8280-6 (sc)
ISBN: 978-1-5127-8279-0 (e)

Library of Congress Control Number: 2017905313

Print information available on the last page.

WestBow Press rev. date: 06/01/2017

CONTENTS

DEDICATION

First, I would like to dedicate this book to my wife of fifty three and half years before God called her home to be with Jesus. Also, I want to dedicate it to my three children and their spouses. Also, I would like to dedicate it to my grandchildren and great grandchildren.

A special thanks goes to my daughter, Letha, and to a teacher friend for helping to edit the manuscript.

SPECIAL NOTE

Roy has hundreds of slides of the places that he visited in Europe while he was in the Army. He transferred the slides to the computer and could refer to them when he wrote about a specific place.

CHAPTER 1

R oy's journey of life began on June 4, 1934, in a coal mining camp in Packard, Kentucky which no longer exists. The morning was very warm and Dr. Rosenberg, the camp doctor, had already delivered one baby boy that morning. This was the tenth baby to Eliza and Elias Vandigrit. Elias worked in the Mahan Jellico Coal Co. coal mine that was owned by a man who lived in a nearby town. The sun had been up for several hours and the doctor was beginning to perspire as he walked along the slate road arriving at the home to find Elias was the only other person there because the children were sent to the neighbors while the baby was being born. It was not long before the child came into the world. The baby boy was named Roy David because his sister wanted him named Roy after her boyfriend, and Gertrude, a very close friend of Eliza, wanted him named David after King David in the Bible.

When Roy was born, his oldest brother, Elmer, who was born on July 4, 1911, was married and lived in Cincinnati, Ohio. Elmer had a one year old daught⁻ The second child, Claude, born on August 3, 1914 in the Civilian Conservation Corps in Camp At⁻

Indiana. Roy's first recollection of Claude was when he came home from the Conservation Corps. His oldest sister, Helen, was born on August 7, 1919, was attending a nearby school, where she graduated from high school and a semester of college before going to Ohio. Then, there was Alice born January, 27, 1923. Jennifer was born December. 17, 1926, and Eugene was born May 14, 1929, still at home. Two years after Roy was born, Jay was born on September 6, 1936, and on December 12, 1937, Elijah was born. There had been one sister and two brothers who had died in infancy.

Roy's ancestry on his father's side is traced as far back as 1652 to John Vandergrit of Guernsey Isle, England and to Hannah Nicholas in 1685 in Middlesex, Virginia. His great grandfather was Richard Witt Vandergrit, and his great grandmother was Emma Vandergrit who were married April 6, 1852, in Anderson County, Tennessee. Grandfather Richard served in the Civil War with Company C, 2nd Tennessee Cavalry. To this couple was born six children which included a set of twins with one of them dying and the brother was Roy's grandfather Richard, who died in January 1941. His grandfather married Roy's grandmother, Judith Roberts, who was born on May 10, 1861, and died July 5, 1949.

Roy's ancestry on his mother's side can be traced back to England. His great grandmother was Wilma Campbell who married Floyd Stanfield. His grandmother's name on his mother's side was Rebecca Stanfield who married Arthur nderson whose father John Anderson had migrated from many and settled in Ironton, Ohio. His grandfather in Pleasant View, Kentucky, in Whitley County.

The first house that Roy remembers living in was across the narrow road from the Packard Baptist Church. There was space in the yard for his parents to grow a garden.

Turnips were his favorite vegetable. He would go to the turnip patch to get them to eat raw. His sister told him that if the family missed him that they could find him in the turnip patch. His family moved into a larger house which had four rooms downstairs and two rooms upstairs and was close to the school. Because this was a mining camp, the coal company owned all the houses. There was no running water into the homes, so a community pump furnished water to be consumed by the families; however, there was a bath house for the miners to take showers to wash off the coal dust from the mines. Also, the male children could use the bath house to bathe.

Packard was a segregated camp. While black families lived on one hillside, the white families lived in the valley and on the other hillsides. In spite of the segregated housing, Roy's mother had several black women friends that would visit in each other's homes and go wild greens picking to cook and eat. His dad had black friends who shared hog killing time. Also, the older children had black friends that visited each other and shared books to read.

When the mine worked out and everyone moved from the camp, one of Roy's mom's black friends who had moved to Tennessee, rode the train to Rockhold and walked the three and half miles to visit his mother. Then, after the visit Roy's dad took her back to the train depot in a wagon for the return trip home. Another black friend, Mrs. Foster, moved to Williamsburg. Sometimes his mother and Mrs. Foster would meet in town and greet each other like long lost friends. When Roy's mother went home to be with the Lord, Mrs. Foster came to the funeral home to pay her respect for his mother.

On August 2, 1937, Roy's grandfather, Arthur Anderson, went home to be with the Lord. His body was laid out in the home as was the custom in those days. There was a large crowd with several children. One day, during the wake, James Anderson, an older cousin, was pulling some of the younger children in a wagon who were making a great deal of noise. He kept telling them to be quiet to no avail. He finally just said to them that if they couldn't be quiet that he would stop pulling them, and that he did to the disappointment of the children.

In the late winter or early spring of about 1938 or 1939, Roy's mother received word that her brother, Estill, had been shot and killed by the Whitley County Sheriff. There had been some kind of trouble when the sheriff got involved. Someone gave him the description of a car that matched Estill's auto. Apparently, Estill did not stop when the sheriff signaled him to stop. Therefore, the sheriff shot and killed him. Roy only remembers that when his mother returned from the funeral that she talked about how cold her friend's car was because it did not have a heater, or it was broken. Estill left a wife, a young daughter, about 4 or 5 years old, and a younger son. Later, the wife married another man and moved to Cincinnati, Ohio. Roy did not see the family again until 1951, when he went to Cincinnati to stay with his sister and only lived a few blocks from where the family lived.

In July 1939, when school started Roy who was only

five years old, asked his mother to let him go to school. She talked to the first grade teacher, Elizabeth Maine, and she agreed to let him come. On August 2, his grandmother Anderson went home to be with the Lord. Therefore, His mother had to take him out of school to take him with her to Pleasant View to be with her family during the time of mourning. While he was there, his mother let him go to the cemetery to watch the men dig his grandmother's grave with picks and shovels. Roy does not remember going to either his grandfather's or grandmother's funeral but assumes that it was in a local Baptist Church that his great uncle helped to start and was the first pastor. Because of the length of absence from school, Roy did not return to class.

In the spring of 1939 or 1940, Jennifer went to Pleasant View to spend the weekend with her cousin Ruth Anderson. One night, there was a popular musical person or group that was performing at the high school building that they attended. After the program ended, they were walking back home along US 25 W when a car swerved off the road and hit them both but never stopped. The accident caused injuries to both of them. After Jennifer came home, she spent several days in the bed under the care of the camp doctor. It is unclear how long Ruth was in the bed. Jennifer never complained about any effects of the accident. The sheriff and others did look for the driver, but he was never found. The driver could have been a local driver, or he could have been a traveler because the highway at that time was one of the major highways from Michigan to Florida.

In July 1940, Roy entered the first grade at the Packard School which was a company school that held grades 1-8. Flora Moses who had married his mother's first cousin, George Moses, was his first grade teacher. The school had two rooms on the first floor and two rooms on the second floor. Sometimes someone would show a black and white movie at night. One movie that Roy remembers was The Three Musketeers. He could never understand how the characters could talk because he didn't know that the film had a sound track until years later. The school was an independent school that began in July and ended in December.

One day, when Jennifer was attending school, she was bent over as the bell was ringing, and the bell clapper came loose and hit her on the head, but God protected her from being seriously injured

There were four people that he remembers from his first grade in 1940. One of them was William whose father was the bookkeeper for the coal company. Shortly after school ended in December 1940, William's family moved to Williamsburg, Kentucky, where his father became the bookkeeper for an automobile dealership. Because the Williamsburg school system had nine months, and William had already passed to the second grade, he was placed in the second grade. Then, he was passed on to the third grade for the following year. Therefore, he got ahead of Roy in school.

The second friend he remembers was Roger who shared the same birthday with Roy. Roy doesn't know to where his family moved when the mine worked out and every one moved from the camp; however, while living in Newport, Kentucky, he met one of Roger's aunts who told him that Roger lived in Northern Kentucky close to the Cincinnati airport. In the early 1960's, a mutual friend took Roy to meet Roger in Erlanger, Kentucky. Roger died not long after that and his wife married one of Roy's former landlords in Newport, Kentucky, whose wife was deceased.

The third person that Roy remembers was Daniel who was the son of one Roy's distant cousins. His family moved to Williamsburg, Kentucky. His father became the owner of a coal mine in Whitley County. Daniel became a prominent ophthalmologist in the Southwest. His mother was a sister to Roy's Uncle Ben's wife, Leona.

The fourth person that he remembers was Josie. After school was out for the year, Josie was playing in the woods near her home and was killed when a log rolled over her. Roy's mother was an excellent seamstress and made Josie's burial dress.

In the summer of 1940, Elmer came for a few days and took his mother, his six year old daughter, Eliza, Jay, Timmy, and Roy to Powell, Tennessee, to see their grandmother. Elmer's automobile only had one seat for the driver and another passenger, possibly two, in the front where he and his mother holding Timmy were seated. The other three were in the rumble seat in the back of the automobile. The trip was going very well until a rain storm came. Elmer stopped the car under a railroad underpass and had the children hunker down. He closed the trunk lid so the children wouldn't get wet. He drove on and when it stopped raining, he stopped and opened the lid. Every time that Roy goes through that area, he thinks about that old incident. On the return trip home, he came by Norris Dam which was on the Clench River and was completed in 1936 to help control floods and provide electricity.

Because the train track was at the end of their yard, one of Roy's favorite past times was to watch the coal burning, steam engine push the empty cars behind the tipple to be ready for loading more coal. Then, the engine would switch to the loaded coal cars on another track to pull them away from the tipple area. Also, there was a Baptist Church across the road that he sometimes attended. At night, if he became sleepy while in church, he would walk back to the house and go to bed. An event that was somewhat scary to a 5 year old was one night, during the invitation, the preacher jumped over the seats to witness to a man. One of the songs that Roy remembers singing was *When the Roll is Called up Yonder* that was written by James Black in 1897 according to a site on internet. Roy went with his sister and some of her friends to visit the black church which was a holiness type church. At one point in the services, the congregation became so "spirit filled" that some of them began to roll on the floor. Because of this type of action, the church was known as Holy Rollers.

Roy can only remember two Christmases at Packard. One Christmas, his mother was sick and unable to cook the holiday dinner, but his sisters cooked the meal for the family; however, a black lady, friend of his mother, brought his mother a Christmas dinner that consisted of turkey, dressing, and other items.

The last Christmas in Packard was in 1940. Roy's dad took one of Roy's siblings through some woods above their house to a farm, where he had been at one time, to cut a Christmas tree. When Roy discovered where they had gone, he thought he knew the way, and without telling his mother, he started to follow them. Before he was halfway there, he met them on their return home with the tree. Since that time, he wonders if he really knew the way or not, and that it was God protecting him from getting lost in the woods. He still has not lost the curiosity of finding short cuts when he is going somewhere. Roy's curiosity led him into a corn field when driving from Cynthiana, Kentucky to Lexington, Kentucky.

That Christmas Roy had gotten a red wagon with which to play. Then one day, he was riding it down a hill when he ran into some obstacle and broke the axle. This was a major disaster for him because the wagon could not be repaired. Not long after that, he was with his brother, Eugene, and some others who were digging for something. Roy ran behind Eugene just as he swung the mattock backward, and it him in the forehead. The accident wasn't too serious and as Roy grew the scar went away.

As a child, his conception of things like other children was limited to what he already knew. Many times the coal mine was referred to as a coal bank. Therefore, when he overheard his parents talking about going to Williamsburg to the bank to make a transaction, his mind envisioned them going back into something like a coal mine to do their business. It wasn't until a month or two later when he went into Williamsburg with his mother to see the Bank of Williamsburg that he realized what a bank was in reality.

It was about in 1939 or 1940 when Roy caught the whooping cough and remembers how hard he coughed. About ten days later, his two younger brothers had the disease. In that time period, there was no medicine to help cure the disease or ease the pain. It just had to run its course.

After his grandmother, Rebecca Anderson, passed away on August 25, 1939, his mother inherited part of the estate which was divided between the heirs. With this money, his parents bought a farm in Whitley County Kentucky. The farm had been part of a much larger one that had been subdivided between members of one family. This farm had been sold to two different families before his parents bought the farm. After moving onto the farm, they bought an adjoining farm that had a log cabin on it from a brother of the woman who had owned their farm and had been part of the larger farm. These two farms made a total of about sixty-five acres.

When Roy's grandfather Vandergrit went to be with the Lord on January 22, 1941, Roy doesn't remember how they traveled there, but Alice went with their dad to the funeral in Powel, Tennessee.

When Roy was about five years old, the miners were on a strike against the coal company. He heard his dad talk about a group of strike suporters that were coming into the camp to aid the strikers. Someone had said that machine guns were set up in the upstairs of the commissary and other places in the camp. When the strike supporters came in trucks, they turned around and left. About that time Roy's dad came from the woods where he had been hunting. An authority arrested him and took him to the jail in Williamsburg where he spent the night. When the authorities learned that he was only hunting and meant no harm to others, they released him from jail.

CHAPTER 2

O n March 22, 1941, Roy's family moved to the farm in Walden, Kentucky, also known as Buffalo. The name of the community was Buffalo, but when the community was provided with a post office there was already another Buffalo in Kentucky. It is conjectured that the Postal Department named the post office after the last man who owned the property whose last name was Walden. But the post office has been removed and all mail comes from another post office. The name of the first postmaster was Mr. Hall. By the time that the Vandergrit family moved to the farm, Mr. Jackson was the postmaster and continued to be the postmaster until he resigned. During World War II, his three sons were in the military, and Mr. Jackson with his wife went to Detroit, Michigan, to work in a factory that aided the efforts of World War II. Mr. Jackson had a battery powered radio that he probably only used to listen to the news for the war situation,

After Mr. Jackson resigned from being the postmaster, Roy's mother became the postmaster and moved the post office to their house where it remained until her death in December 1960. Her son, Claude, who had bought the property from Mr. Jackson became the postmaster and moved the post office back to the building where the store was.

Buffalo Elementary School had only one room with the first grade through the eighth grade and two teachers. Legend has the school dating before the Civil War and high school subjects were taught there. During the second grade, Miss Morgan was his teacher. She taught the first through the fourth grade while her father, Mr. Andy Morgan, taught the fifth through the eighth grade. Sadly, shortly after the end of the school year, Mr. Morgan died from a brain hemorrhage while being transported by an ambulance from Pineville to Lexington. Miss Griffey was his third grade teacher while Mrs. Cox was the other teacher. She was the only teacher for all eight grades during his fourth grade year. Mr. Taylor, who lived in the community, was the only teacher for the school his fifth through the eighth grade years. Mr. Taylor's oldest son, Felix, was Roy's age and in the same grade. Also, he had a younger son, Blain.

Mr. Taylor, had an accident when he was young and lost one of his legs above his knee. As a result, he had a prosthesis. Everyone in the community called it a wooden leg. Because he lived about two miles from school, he would ride a mule to school and keep it in Roy's brother's barn. Mr. Taylor paid Roy to sweep the school and build the fire in the potbelly stove that was in the room. Sometimes the stove pipe would get red hot all the way to the brick chimney that went out past the roof. One morning, one of the boys threw some 22 rifle shells in the stove. They just made a loud noise when they exploded. Most of the older boys carried a knife to school and nothing was ever said about it. Also, some of the older boys and Mr. Taylor would go to the outside toilet to smoke.

Mr. Taylor loved baseball and would travel to Cincinnati, Ohio, to watch the Cincinnati Reds play. During the lunch hour, the students would choose two ball captains and they would choose other students to be on their sides to play baseball. Mr. Taylor would be on one side, and he was a great hitter with just his right arm, but he couldn't run. He usually chose Roy to run for him because Roy was considered a fast runner. The church was so close in proximity to the school, that a good hitter could break a window pane with a home run. Roy was not a very good ball player because he couldn't hit the ball very far and usually was one of the last ones to be chosen for a team.

Sometimes Mr. Taylor would take as many students who wanted to walk to another school on Friday afternoons to play that school's baseball team. The team might be as far as three miles away. The away teams were Shiner, Tidal Wave, Holly Marsh, and Cripple Creek. Since there was no bus transportation, all of these schools required about an hour of walking. If any of the students didn't want to go to the away games, Mr. Taylor would let them go home for the rest of the day. In the winter, when only a few students attended school, he would send a couple of students to the store to buy each student a soft drink of their choice and have all the lessons in the morning and dismiss the afternoon classes.

Other games students played were Base, Fox and Dog, Tag, and Anne Over.

To play Base, two captains took turns choosing the students who wanted to play into two groups. Then, a long line drown on the ground or an old log was used as a base with a circle drawn at one end to hold the students of the opposing side when they were tagged. Each team member would stand on the line then venture as close to the other team as they dared without being tagged by a member of the other team before getting back to base. If the person was tagged, he or she would have to go stand in the ring. Fox and Dog was played almost the same way. To play Annie Over, the students divided in two groups. One group would go on one side of the school and the other group would go on the other side of the school. Then, a student from one team would throw a ball over the school to the other side. Then, the teams would try to change sides without being tagged by a student from the opposite side. If a student were tagged, that person had to go to the other team. The side that had the most students at the end of the game was the winner.

The school and grounds served as a meeting place for the young people in the community to gather on a Sunday afternoon to socialize, or play baseball, or basketball when the weather permitted. The school had no electricity or running water, but there was a well on the school property. A dipper was used to fill the collapsible tin cups or a temporary cup made by folding a sheet of paper in the shape of a cone to hold water. The windows were raised in the hot weather to let the wind blow through the building to help cool it.

One of Roy's favorite subjects in elementary school was geography. In geography, one could learn about how people lived in faraway countries and what their agricultural life was like. This fascinated him because of the rural life in Buffalo. This was Roy's medium to the outside world because there was no electricity in the community. Also, there were no telephones, or television. As a matter of fact, Roy never saw television until he was sixteen years old when he went to stay with his sister in Cincinnati. Roy's parents had an electric radio that they used while they lived in Packard, and when the Rural Electric Administration electricity finally came to the community.

There was a book, *If I were Going*, in the Alice and Jerry Basic Reading Program printed by Row, Peterson and Company in 1941. This book was about a railroad depot agent, Mr. Sanders, who retired and the railroad company sent him and his wife on a steamship to Europe to see the many sights of the different countries in Europe.

At that time Roy could only dream about going to these places because he didn't know what God had in store for his future. He did not know then, that years later he would find himself on a ship going to see many of the places that he had read about in this third grade book. Of course the circumstances were much different than just reading about the places because he was in the United States Army on a troop ship, the United States Navy Ship Upshur.

In September of 2012, one of Roy's nephews told him that he had learned that the first recording of Gospel music was made by a quartet from Buffalo. Their picture and a song could be found on the internet under Buffalo Ragged Five, but there are only four men, Mr.

Jackson, Mr. Morgan, Mr. Parson, and Mr. Edmond. Roy supposes the fifth was Mr. Parson's guitar. Roy found this very fascinating since he knew them and their families except Mr. Edmond who lived in Corbin. He knew who Edmond was because his sister was Roy's neighbor and taught him for one year in Sunday school. Mr. Edmond died at an early age and left a young child that his sister and her husband, partially raised after they moved to Corbin, Kentucky. Jack Taylor returned to Kentucky after he retired in Michigan and went to be with the Lord probably in the late sixties or early seventies. Mr. Parson has gone to his heavenly home. Mr. Morgan is the same one mentioned earlier.

After moving to the farm, Roy's father continued to work in the Packard coal mine. During the week he stayed in a boarding house that was operated by Roy's great aunt, Beth Anderson. The only public transportation to Packard was when the train brought a combine car which took passengers and freight to Savoy. His dad had to find other means to come home. Sometimes he would get a ride from Packard to Williamsburg, then catch a bus to Rockhold and walk the three and half miles on home. Other times, he would walk or catch a mine motor car through the mountain and walk to US Highway 25 to catch a bus to Williamsburg and on to Rockhold and then, walk on home. Roy never heard his dad complain that it was a hardship for him.

In 1942, Roy's dad went to Powell and brought his 81 year old mother to live with the family. Roy's Grandmother Vandergrit had a reputation of being contrary and hard to get along with other people. Someone said that she had broken his grandfather's arm. She would not eat the biscuits and cornbread that Mom Vandergrit would bake, but she said the only bread that she could eat was store bought bread. Many times someone would walk three and half miles each way to purchase the bread for her, but Eliza said that she would see Grandmother take her biscuits and hide them to eat later. Roy's dad said that she hid his hammer from him, and he couldn't find it for a long time. On one occasion, one of Roy's sisters made some pies. After they were baked, Grandma Vandergrit took them out of the pans and set them on newspapers that made a print on the pies. That did not go over very well with his sister. At night, when she would go to bed, she would talk to herself saying things about the family. Finally, she got so bad that Roy's dad had to get his brother-in-law to move her back to her home in Powell where she had two sons and a daughter who could watch after her. One of the sons owned and operated a store close by where she lived. One of Roy's aunts said to him, "If Eliza couldn't get along with your grandmother, she really must have been bad."

After World War II began, the government rationed many things such as coffee, and kerosene that was used for the lamps. Any kind of meat was difficult to find. At one point, Roy's mother heard there was going to be a store about four miles from their house that would have bacon that she wanted to use to season her cooked food. She sent the three youngsters to the store, but when they arrived the meat was all gone. On their way back home, a heavy thunder storm came. The three sought shelter in a barn that was close to the road, but they were sopping wet by the time they entered the barn. Also, during the war, Roy's dad bought him a pair of shoes that had soles made from recycled car tires.

Claude worked in the mine at Packard, and when the mine worked out, he moved to Garmeda, or Log Mont, Kentucky which is in Bell County close to Middlesboro, to work in the mine. Roy's dad stayed with Claude and his family and worked there for a time.

While Roy's dad was working at Garmeda, there was an accident that broke his arm. The doctor who treated him had to put bars in both parts of the broken bone and then connected them with another bar. During this time his dad developed rheumatism in one of his thighs. The doctor had him to make his own concoction of liniment. Some of the ingredients were eggs, turpentine, and alcohol, along with other items. The mixture smelled horrible, but apparently it helped the rheumatism. Later, he found work in a mine at Rockhold where he could walk about five miles to work. Since he worked nights, he didn't get home until after midnight.

One winter, Eugene was very sick, and all the home remedies were not making him any better. Roy's dad rode a horse three and half miles through the rain to Rockhold where the nearest telephone was to call a doctor to come to the house. After calling the doctor, he had to wait for the doctor to come from Corbin to Rockhold. The road was so muddy and bad that the doctor could not drive the distance on to Buffalo. Roy's dad let the doctor ride the horse on to the house. After seeing Eugene and giving him some medicine, Roy's dad let the doctor ride the horse back to Rockhold while he walked to ride the horse back home. Eugene did get well which was a blessing, but he did not accept Christ until later in life after he married his second wife.

When Roy was in the eighth grade, he caught the measles. He broke out all over with a rash and had headaches and a fever. The only things to ease his misery were cold wash clothes on his head and lying in the bed. It seemed like an eternity before he felt well enough to get up and stir about. The next week his friend had a birthday party and invited him. He returned home through a cold rain. As a result, he had a "back set" which was worse than the measles. Not only did he have the headache and fever, but he had a very bad ear ache.

There was a 4-H Club at Buffalo that was an organization from the Kentucky Agriculture Department. The 4-H stands for head, heart, hands, and health. Roy's mother was the local sponsor. The club had a president that presided over the meetings. There was a secretary that recorded the events of the meetings and then sent the report to the Whitley Republican newspaper. This was an agricultural organization, so the members had to have some sort of project related to agriculture. For instance, one could take gardening and keep a record of the cost of planting the garden, the kind of vegetables grown and crop yield. One year, Roy took chickens as his project. His dad built a small chicken house to hold the one hundred baby chickens that were ordered from the University of Kentucky and were sent by parcel post. The cost of feed and other expenses had to be recorded until they grew into full grown chickens.

There was a 4-H Club Camp in the summer that consisted of clubs from several counties at Levi Jackson

State Park in Laurel County. In order to go to camp, the member was assigned to bring an allotted number of vegetables that were to be used at the camp. The assignment might be 1 head of cabbage, twelve carrots, a peck of potatoes, and other vegetables and some money to purchase perishable items. Roy was able to go to the camp for two summers. He had to walk carrying all these items plus a pillow and sheets, for three and half miles to meet the extension agent to take him on to Levi Jackson State Park. Instructors taught many subjects about farming and how to raise different kinds of farm crops. Someone taught how to judge cows and other animals to determine the best of two or more. There would be games and other forms of entertainment. One night, a pillow fight was started by a couple of boys and soon escalated into many other joining the fight. After it was over, Roy went home with a different pillow than he brought from home.

About 1947, Roy had a boil to come on his arm between the elbow and wrist. At first, a home remedy poultice of Epson Salts was used, but the infection grew to the point that his mother had to pay someone in the community to take him to Dr. Eversole in Williamsburg. After he examined the arm and wrapped it, he picked up a phone that had a direct line to the drug store to call in a prescription for Roy to take. The only other time that Roy had gone into town for medical treatment was when he had an abscessed tooth that couldn't be treated at home and had to be pulled by a dentist. However, the children did go to the Whitley County Health department to take shots to prevent typhoid fever.

When students were in the eighth grade, they were given a standardized test to determine if they were qualified to go to high school. When the proctor came to school, Roy was sick with the measles and was unable to take the test. The school superintendent allowed him to come to his office and take the test which he passed and was allowed to enter Rockhold High School for the1948-1949 school year. If a student did not pass the eighth grade test, the student could enter high school on a six weeks trial period. If the student failed any subjects, the student had to drop out of high school. There were about seventy-five students in his freshman class, but by the junior year, only fifteen were left. At that time, the law was that a student only had to go to school until completing the eighth grade or until reaching their sixteenth birthday. Many students did not go any further than the eighth grade. Some students turned sixteen years of age before completing the eighth grade and dropped out of school. Transportation was a problem for students who lived in places where a school bus did not run to take them to a high school.

When Roy was a freshman in high school, the transportation was in the backend of a truck that was owned by the principal of the school and lived in Buffalo. The truck bed had benches in it and a tarpaulin for the cover. The principal would pick up the students who lived in Buffalo at the store and then pick up students on the way to the school. Needless to say, in the winter time the bed of the truck would be very cold for the fifteen minutes or so that it took to go the four miles to school.

The next two years the transportation was in a vehicle that had been a former bread truck. It was about the size of a minivan without any windows. There was a bench on both sides of the vehicle which had to make two trips to accommodate all the students from first grade through the seniors in high school. For the 1951-1952 school year, a small school bus was used. Roy did not go to Rockhold that year for reasons discussed later in the book, but his two younger brothers did.

The school was built around the gymnasium with eight class rooms. The elementary grades one through eight occupied four of the rooms on one side of the gym and each class of the high school occupied the other rooms on the other side of the gym. The school had been built by the Workers Progressive Administration, which was an organization that was under President Franklin D. Roosevelt's administration to create jobs after the Great Depression in the 1930's. There were only four teachers for the entire high school. One teacher was for English, one for math, one for the sciences, and one for history and geography. One of the teachers was the principal of the high school and the principal of the eight elementary grades. During the junior year, a typing and bookkeeping teacher, Mr. Baker, was added and taught on the stage. Roy took the typing class that proved very beneficial to him when he was inducted into the Army. Mr. Baker had been in World War II and had what was then called Shell Shock, but now it is called Post Traumatic Stress Disorder.

During Roy's freshman year, polio was a nationwide epidemic proportion and a girl in the first grade came down with that horrible disease that killed many people and left many others crippled for life. The school was closed for about a week while health officials decontaminated it. That girl grew to be a woman and is still living as of this writing in 2017. A friend told Roy that she was at the last school reunion that he attended in 2013, but he didn't recognize her.

One day, when Roy went to one of the stores in Rockhold to get lunch, he saw a lady who was pushing a wheelbarrow with her young son come through the community. She had started her journey somewhere in Florida and was pushing the wheelbarrow across America to Michigan. He has often wondered if she made it all the way and what ever happened to her son.

The family across the narrow road from the school had a cocker spaniel dog that would howl every day for a few minutes after one o'clock while a Louisville and Nashville passenger train going south was passing through Rockhold. Of course, the students thought this was amusing and would laugh. One afternoon, after the train had gone through the community, the mother of one of the students came to the school to get the student. She told him that his grandfather had been killed by the train. The grandfather, who was a minister, had been suffering from depression and had only been home a few days from a mental institution. When he heard the train coming, he put his glasses on the mantel and walked across the highway onto the tracks in front of the train.

There were two big events his junior year. One was in the fall 0f 1950 when the seniors and juniors made a field trip to Mammoth Cave and My Old Kentucky Home. The other event was in the spring when there was a Junior-Senior Banquet at the Cumberland Falls State Park DuPont Lodge.

Basketball was the only sport that required playing other schools. Because the school was so small, and the pool of players was small the team did not win many games. All four county high schools in Whitley County were small.

Both Williamsburg City School and Corbin City School had football teams. Roy never saw a football game until he was seventeen years old in Cincinnati when his cousin invited him to see one of her school's game. Watching the game was very boring to him because it was like an old song "What It Was – Was Football". Football games are still boring to him, but he did attend them when his children played in the band in high school and college. Also, when he would go to see his grandchildren and they would be involved with them in some way.

One night, Roy was riding with his principal, Mr. Wells, and one of the basketball players to a game in Pleasant View. As they were passing the house where one of Roy's uncles and his family including his cousin lived, he said, "There is where my uncle lives."

The ballplayer said, "There is where my aunt lives." Then, he told Roy that he had stayed with them the past year and had gone to Pleasant View High School during his junior year, Roy's cousin who now lives in Michigan and Roy continue to keep in touch with each other. The cousin reminds Roy about that incident when they meet at funerals or family reunions. Both Rockhold and Pleasant View high schools no longer exist because all the county high schools were consolidated into one high school.

CHAPTER 3

G rowing up on a farm was not always easy. It meant that farm work was done on the coldest days as well as the hottest days of the year. After moving to the farm, the family had to adjust to kerosene lighting because electricity did not come to the community until the summer of 1947. When the Rural Electric Administration strung electric lines to transmit the electricity, the electric poles were dragged by horses to the posthole that had been dug with a hand posthole digger. The post had to be installed by hand. A horse would pull the electric line beyond the pole. The installer would climb the pole and attach the line to the pole. The process would be repeated until the line was completed.

Roy's father hired electricians to wire the house for electricity but had to wait for the inspector to come to inspect the wiring and wait until someone came to install the electric meter to turn on the electricity. On the day that the electricity was turned on, Roy, his dad, and two younger brothers had been working out of sight of the house on another part of the farm. It was almost dark when they came in view of the house and saw that the electricity had been turned on. Those lights seemed to be the brightest lights that they had ever seen. What a blessing it was to have electric lights and to hear the radio again.

Roy's first chore on the farm was that of a water boy. He was responsible during the summer, when his brother and sisters or others worked in the fields, to carry fresh water from the well in a used gallon lard bucket to the workers. The Vandergrit's well water was one of the best tasting waters in the community and never ran dry or got low in the summer as many other wells did in dry weather.

As Roy got older, he learned other farm chores. One of the chores was to plant the seed corn and other seeds. As the corn grew, either his brother, Eugene, or his dad would use a four footed cultivating plow to plow the corn or tobacco to cut the weeds between the rows. When the garden was too wet to plow, Roy and his two younger brothers would have to pull the weeds from the garden. In the fall, when the corn was ready to be picked, Roy's dad, Roy, and his brothers had to pull the corn from the stalk and put it in a wagon to be taken to the crib which was inside the barn. The corn stalks were cut and shocked for fodder to be fed to the livestock. Sometimes the leaves were pulled from the corn stalks and tied in bundles then shocked. On some occasions that process would be done at night when lanterns were used to see. One year a neighbor had Roy's dad to raise a corn crop on a steep hillside on a share basis. That fall when they had the wagon about half full, it turned over in the field. Of course, it was a chore to get the wagon back in the upright position and all the corn put back in the wagon.

Another summer time chore was to pick blackberries

for Roy's mother to can in quart jars. All who picked berries usually got chiggers that would cause them to itch. One of the neighbors reported that he heard Roy's brother praying to God that He would fill his bucket. Sometimes Roy would see a snake in the berry bushes and that is when he went somewhere else to pick berries. The berries were certainly delicious in the winter when his mom made blackberry cobblers or just to eat with hot biscuits and sugar. Picking berries was a very good excuse to go to the swimming hole for a swim to wash away the chiggers.

Roy's father had a small tobacco allotment which meant that the tobacco had to be raised. In those days, the first step in growing tobacco was to burn a pile of brush on an area about eight or ten feet wide and twenty feet long to kill all the weed seeds. The next step was to sow the tobacco seeds in the bed where the brush was burned. Because the tobacco seeds were so small, they were mixed with fertilizer to spread over the bed. A type of cheese cloth was spread over the bed about ten inches high to let the plants grow without getting bit by an early frost. By the time the plants were big enough to transplant, it was warm enough to move them to the tobacco field. Setting them out was a family chore of hand setting them. The tobacco had to be hoed to keep the weeds from over taking the plants. When the blooms grew on the plants, they had to be topped (cut from the plant). After the tobacco was topped, suckers grew on the plants and had to be pulled from the tobacco stalk. Soon after this, the tobacco turned yellow, or ripened, and had to be cut. His dad would usually cut the tobacco while the boys were in school, but he depended on his sons to help him hang the tobacco in the barn and the log cabin. This meant that the plants were cut and put on four feet sticks for them to be put on tiers in a barn to cure, dry, and turn brown. It was difficult for Roy to reach down to grasp the sticks of tobacco and raise above his head to the next person to hang on the beams to dry.

Another fall job was to harvest the two kinds of potatoes. First, there was the Irish potatoes which Roy's dad would turn out of the soil with a plow. Then, Roy and his two younger brothers would pick them up and put them in a pile, or lay them out of the way, so that the plow could go the other direction. After the potatoes were cured for a short time, they would be stored in the cellar to be eaten during the winter. They would last until the next summer when enough of the new potatoes for a meal could be taken without disturbing the growth of the rest of the new potatoes.

The cellar had been constructed by a previous owner who was afraid of storms. It had been dug out of the hillside. The walls were made with rocks and concrete approximately eight feet high, twelve feet wide, twenty-five feet long and about eight to ten inches thick with a six inch thick flat roof made of concrete. There was an air vent on each side. There were bins in the side bottom and backend of the cellar to store potatoes and shelves above the bins to store jars of canned vegetables and fruit. The opposite side had a small stove with a pipe going out of the top and a large bench for a mattress. When a storm was coming, the owner would go to the cellar and stay until the storm had passed.

The second kind of potato was the sweet potatoes or yams which took more preparation to plant. The sweet potatoes were started by setting out sweet potato plants that had been started in a "hot bed". The hot bed was made by digging out a shallow plot of ground and partially filling it with a layer of manure from the barn. Then, a layer of sawdust would be added. Several sweet potatoes would be placed on this, and then, several inches of sawdust would be placed on the sweet potatoes. Finally, a cover would be placed a few inches above the sawdust to cover the bed. The potatoes would sprout and grow under the cover. When there was no longer any danger of frost, the cover would be removed to let the plants acclimate to the sun. The plants or slips would be pulled and reset in ridges of soil that had been made by pulling the dirt into a ridge several inches high. Naturally, they would have to be cultivated to keep the weeds from choking them. Before they were harvested the long vines had to be cut from them. They were harvested the same way as the Irish Potatoes but were cured on top of the cellar for two or three days and then stored in a pit of sawdust under the house. These made for excellent eating when they were seasoned with pork grease and baked or fried.

Roy's mother and sisters would can many jars of fruits and vegetables to be eaten during the winter months. One time a snake got in the cellar and Roy was afraid to go in it because he was so afraid of snakes. Another time the cellar door was left open and the cow entered the cellar. She got her head stuck in one of the potato bins. Because Roy's father was not home at that time, one of the neighbors came and sawed off part of the bin support to free the cow.

When the Vandergrit family first moved into their two bedroom, kitchen, dining room, and living room home, the house was heated with a fireplace in the living room. There was not much heat that circulated into the other rooms unless the kitchen stove was being used to cook and helped to heat the back room. The chimney was made on the outside of the house so that the ashes could be dropped from the grate down to the outside through the lower part of the chimney. At this time, Roy's dad was away working in the mine during the week. One night, his Mom woke everyone and said that the house was on fire. Immediately, water was drawn from the well and put on the fire to extinguish it. Then, it was discovered that one of the hot coal embers had gotten stuck on a floor joist that had not been completely covered with whatever was used to fireproof the chimney.

After this incident, Roy's dad bought a Warm Morning heater which could burn either, or both, coal or wood. Sometimes his dad would buy several tons of coal, and sometimes the coal would be supplemented with wood. Other times he would decide to use only wood. When wood was decided upon, his dad, three brothers, and Roy would have to saw the wood about eighteen inches long and split some of it into kindling to start fires. The cook stove used the same kind of fuel. It seemed that regardless of how much fire wood they had at the beginning of winter, on the coldest day of the winter they would run out of cut wood and would have to saw more wood to keep warm and for his mom to cook. His mom would kindle the fire every morning in the kitchen stove to cook breakfast for the family.

There was one drawback with the Warm Morning stove. His dad had to rig the stove pipe to the chimney with a stove elbow pipe that curved down from the top of the heater to about half way down the backside of the stove and use another elbow pipe and a straight three feet piece of straight pipe level to the bricked up fireplace. The straight pipe from the heater would fill with soot and block the draft to the outside. This construction caused the fire to smolder in the heater and fill the room with smoke. After the fire would be extinguished, his dad would have to disassemble the stove pipe, take the pipe outside, and shake out the soot. He would then reassemble the pipe to the chimney. In the meantime the house would cool to a very uncomfortable temperature.

The cook stove was used to heat the irons with which to iron the clothes. On one end of the stove was a water reservoir in which water could be heated and used for taking baths in a large wash tub. During the winter the back bedrooms were very cold, especially the room where Roy slept; however, there were many covers to keep them warm including a feather bed that had belonged to his grandmother Anderson. When the temperature dropped very low, the water in the bucket in the kitchen would freeze. Roy's mom or dad would get up during the night to check the fire in the living room stove to keep it burning during the night

Some of the fun things were playing either baseball or basketball or just socializing in the school yard or on the porch and steps of the school house, where most of the young people gathered on Sunday afternoons in the summer time. After playing and getting hot, most of the boys would hike through the fields to the Sharp's Swimming Hole. The swimming hole was at a wide and deep part of Blake's Fork Creek that runs about three fourths of a mile from the schoolhouse and is one of the boundaries of the Vandergrift's farm. There was a huge flat rock that jutted into the water and made a good place to climb onto and dry off. The water was always cold because a spring ran from under the rock that jutted into the creek. The story went that a couple had been standing under the rock as a shelter when a bad storm came and had just left before it fell. God must have been with that couple.

Another fun thing was the "pie supper" that the school sponsored almost every year. Most of the girls in the community would bake a pie to be auctioned to raise money for the school to buy necessary supplies which the school board did not provide. The object of the auction was to get the girl's boyfriend to buy the pie. Most of the time other boys would run the bid up so that the boyfriend would have to pay more than he wanted to pay for the pie. Also, there might be a contest to see who could guess what an object would be in an unidentified container. Of course, the guessing would cost something and the prize might be a cake or a pie. After the pie supper, the boys had the opportunity to walk the girls to their home lighting the way with a flashlight or a lantern. Almost all the time, a parent was close behind the couple.

Attending church services at the Buffalo Missionary Baptist Church was another thing that Roy enjoyed all year long. The building only had one room with a coal burning potbellied stove in the middle of the room and had kerosene lights that had to be filled and trimmed to keep them burning. There was no piano; therefore, all hymns were sung without any kind of musical instrument. To get the tune and pitch right, the song leader would use a tuning fork to set the tone. The notes were shaped notes and sometimes there would be a "singing school" to learn how to read and sing the shaped notes. The church changed pastors every year or two. The church was considered a part time church. Services were held on the second and fourth Saturday nights and the following Sunday mornings because some of the preachers had to travel from out of the community to be there and held another job during the week. Sometimes one of the men in the community would have to drive to the pastor's home a few miles away to bring him to the church.

The church had a revival in the spring and again in August that would have services in the morning and at night. If the students in school wanted to go to church during school hours, the teacher, Mr. Taylor, would permit them to attend the services. The ones who accepted Christ during the revival were baptized in a creek about a mile from the church. To get to the creek the congregation had to walk most of the way. Part of the way was a narrow dirt road, and the rest of the way was on a narrow path that was beside a small branch of water. Sometimes a farm pond would be used for the baptism. Of course, Roy heard evangelists preach that if a person is not saved when that person dies that Hell is the destination, but if one does accept Christ as a personal savior, Heaven is their destination. By the time Roy was eleven or twelve years old, he felt the Lord dealing with him but kept procrastinating about accepting Christ.

After the baptismal services in August of 1947, Roy was walking back from the services with the preacher who held the revival. He told Roy that he should accept Christ as his savior while he was still young and his heart was still tender. That remark stuck in Roy's mind. On January 17, 1948, while in his bed before going to sleep, he accepted Christ into his life when he was thirteen years old. During the revival in April, he made his confession of faith and in May was baptized in Blake's Fork Creek but in a different place than the swimming hole. Roy's brother and two friends were baptized at the same baptismal service led by James Polly, pastor of the Faber Baptist Church, whose baptismal candidates participated in being baptized. There was a saying about baptizing in the creek that is worth repeating, "You can be baptized in the creek so many times that the minnows know you, but if you haven't been saved, baptism won't do you any good."

After Roy became a member of the church, he became the custodian of the church. One duty was to build the fires in the potbellied stove that was in the middle of the one room building. Because there were no phones in the community when a person in the community passed away, someone in the family would go to Roy and tell him the name and age of the one who had passed. Roy would go to the church where he would ring the church bell several times. Then he would toll the bell one time for each year that the deceased person was old. After the people heard the tolling of the bell, some of them would come and ask about the dead person.

One time, several children were playing in Claude's backyard when Roy's mom called him to come home, but he didn't go right away. As he was running in the yard he stepped on a nail and it went into his foot and hurt quite a bit. The Bible verse "Children, obey your parents in the Lord: for this is right. Honor thy father and mother; which is the first commandment with a promise; that it may be well with thee, and thou mayest live long on the earth." Ephesians 6:1-3 KJV, came to his mind and he knew that God was punishing him for not going home when his mother called him. His mother made him soak his foot in Epsom salts water to keep infection from getting into his foot. He did learn a valuable lesson from this experience - to obey his parents.

As the brothers and sisters got old enough to work in public works, they would go north to find a job to earn money for themselves. Elmer was already in Cincinnati working in the Alms Hotel, a very plush hotel in Walnut Hills. He worked there until World War II began, and he began to work for Wright Brothers Manufacturing Company in Avondale, Ohio that produced airplane parts. He was deferred from the draft because he worked in a defense plant. When Claude came home from Camp Atterbury, he started working in the coal mine. He was deferred from the draft because he was a coal miner, and the military needed the coal. The third sibling, Helen, was attending a nearby academy. After one semester of college, she went to Cincinnati where she married Brian Clarkson who was drafted into the Army and spent most of his time in California as a cook. Alice was still at home, but when school began, she started staying with her

Uncle William's wife in Saxton, Kentucky and attended high school. At that time, Jennifer and Eugene were too young to work in public works and were home, and they moved to the farm with the rest of the family. When they got old enough to work at public works, Jennifer went to Cincinnati, Ohio, and Eugene went to Hamilton, Ohio, to find jobs. Both of them only went to the eighth grade. Jennifer and Eugene would send money home to help supplement the family's income after their dad had to quit working in the mine and the small income from Roy's mom being postmaster. When Jennifer and Eugene married they stopped sending money to the parents.

In the spring of 1945, Roy's mother's first cousin's wife came to his dad and asked if he would plant a field of corn on shares. She said that her husband had turned the ground the fall before he passed away late that winter. Roy's dad agreed to plant the field in corn that was on a steep hillside. After the corn was planted, it started to rain and rained off and on until the weeds out grew the corn before it could be cultivated. By the time it could be plowed with a four footed cultivator, long "saw briers" had grown in with other weeds. The sun beat down on all of those who were trying to hoe the corn. While working in the field, the conversation turned to the atomic bomb that was dropped on Japan and how close Oak Ridge, Tennessee was to the community and the secretiveness of the making of the bombs. Being 11 years old, Roy was old enough to handle a hoe to work in the field, which was a very difficult chore for him.

One day, while mom brought their lunch to them, she left Timmy and his brother home by themselves. She was very surprised when she returned home and found that her brother, Perry Anderson, who lived in Perry County close to Hazard, had brought his son, Richard, who at that time was working in Toledo, to visit for a while. He said that his second wife was very difficult to live with and did not like his daughter, Dorothy. One day, she sent him to the post office to mail a letter to Dorothy. He decided to open it, and she had written that Dorothy was not to come and visit her dad anymore and some other bad things. He said that he went to his bank and drew out all of his money. Then, he went to Toledo to bring Richard to Roy's parent's house because they lived three and half miles from the nearest telephone and highway. He thought that she would not be able to find him at the Vandergrit's house. He had not told anyone else where he was. After a few weeks, Roy's uncle Jonathan, his mom's brother, came from Pleasant View to see if she had heard anything about Uncle Perry. He was surprised when he arrived to see him there. Uncle Perry's wife had gone to Uncle Jonathan's home to see if he had heard from Uncle Perry, but Jonathan did not know where Perry was. Jay told Roy that when Uncle Perry first came that Timmy and he did not know who he was and he would not tell them. Timmy told him, "If you don't tell us who you are, I am going to get a gun and shoot you." Now, he was only eight years old and was short of stature. The gun that he was going to use was a ten gauge shot gun and very heavy. Therefore, it is doubtful if he could have managed to load it and fire it.

In the meantime, the cousin's wife had rented her house to another family and had moved to a smaller, older house which was some distance from the smokehouse and cellar. When time came to pick and store the corn, Roy's dad asked the wife where she wanted her share of the corn stored. She said that she wanted to keep it separate from the other corn and that he should put it in a smokehouse that was above a cellar which was near the rented house. About a month after the corn was stored in the smokehouse, the local paper ran a story about the sheriff and revenue officers confiscating a moonshine still from under the smokehouse and arresting the man who lived in the house. Of course, Roy's family teased their dad about abetting the man by putting the corn above the "still."

CHAPTER 4

At the end of Roy's junior year in high school, he realized that his parents did not have the money for him to buy a class ring and to rent the cap and gown to wear when graduating the following year. He went to Cincinnati in April 1951, to live with his sister, Helen, for the summer while he worked where his brother-in-law was able to get him a job at the Western Auto Supply Warehouse which was in St. Bernard, Ohio, next to Cincinnati.

When it was time for school to start in Rockhold, he told his boss that he was going to quit work to return home to finish high school. His boss asked him if he had thought about keeping on working and going to night high school in Cincinnati to get his diploma. It seemed to be a good idea. The only requirement was that he had to get a work permit because he was under eighteen. He continued working and going to West Night High School for the next school year. He would work eight hours during the day and go to school at night for two and half hours for the school year. In June 1952, about two weeks after he turned eighteen he received his high school diploma. In September, he enrolled in the University of

Cincinnati but only attended for one semester that ended in January 1953. Like his brother and sister, he sent money home until his dad started drawing Social Security for himself, Roy's mother, and Roy's two younger brothers.

While working and attending the University of Cincinnati at night, where he took Algebra I and Accounting I, Roy began to have an urge to join the Air Force. He had wanted to be a pilot and the United States was involved in the Korean War. Eugene had been drafted in the Army and was doing duty in Korea. In February 1953, he volunteered for the Air Force, but he did not pass the physical exam. The doctor discovered a heart murmur that Roy didn't know he had. When he asked the doctor what caused the murmur, the doctor replied that he didn't know but recommended a cardiologist, Dr. Greenberg, in Cincinnati who might be able to tell him.

Dr. Greenberg was in the Carew Tower Building on the twenty-second floor. After a fluoroscope and an electrocardiogram, he told Roy that nothing showed up abnormally on either test, but there was another test that he could do. It would have to be done in St. Mary's Hospital in Cincinnati. Roy agreed to the test, but because he was under the age of twenty-one, one of his parents had to sign for him to have the test. The test was a cardiac catheterization and was so new that the American Heart Association paid for it. The Air Force examining doctor assisted Dr. Greenberg with the test and told Roy that he wished that he had what Roy had. When Roy questioned him as to why he said that the problem would never bother Roy but that he would never have to go into the military. The doctor explained that he was in the Navy Reserves and was being called back into active duty. He said that if he had a heart murmur that he would not have to go back to the Navy. Roy felt a bit of sadness in his heart because he knew that he could never be a pilot in the Air Force or never have to go in the service. Little did the doctor or Roy know then that God had other plans for Roy's life.

Not long after Roy went to Cincinnati, he went a few times to the Auburn Avenue Baptist church that no long exists. But he did not feel comfortable in that church. He began to go to a Baptist Church that was farther out of the city than the Auburn Avenue Baptist Church and took much longer to get there by city bus than the Auburn Avenue Baptist Church. Not long after that, he started going with his niece to a Church of the Nazarene that no longer exists where Jennifer had gone before she married her husband. Roy felt very comfortable going there, so that is where he went until his friend from Buffalo came to Norwood, and they started going to the movies every Saturday night. It was not long until he wanted to sleep in and stayed away from church.

During the summer, Roy liked to go to Coney Island, that no longer exists, to ride the rides and go swimming. Coney Island would have nationally known entertainers to come for programs. The entertainment drew large crowds, but it was a segregated place. Even when black entertainers came, the blacks could not attend the program. Roy could not understand that practice.

Events changed one Saturday morning after Roy answered the knock on his door.

The man who was at the door introduced himself as a Sunday school teacher, and told Roy that he was his new

Sunday school teacher at the Church of the Nazarene, that no longer exists. He said that he would come by and take him to Sunday school and church if Roy would let him. So, Roy gladly began attending church and was involved in the young people's activities. One night, before the class was going to have refreshments, the Sunday school teacher asked Roy to say the blessing. He had never prayed in public before. His first thought was Lord, open up the floor and let me drop through it, but he did get through his first short public prayer. Later, he had to change Sunday school classes because of his age. Roy continued to work at the Western Auto Warehouse and attend the Stanton Avenue Church of the Nazarene where he attended for about two and half years.

One Sunday, as Roy was leaving church, the pastor asked, "Roy, when are you going to move your membership to our church?" He didn't have time to answer because his teacher who was standing behind said in amazement, " Roy, you mean that you are not a member of the church?" Roy told them that he would only be there for two more Sundays because he was returning home to attend Cumberland College but now has a different name

CHAPTER 5

R oy began to feel he needed to do something with his life other than working in a warehouse. He felt that he should go back home to attend Cumberland College that was a two year college in Williamsburg, Kentucky that was close to his home, and he could commute to classes. He felt that he needed to teach in Eastern Kentucky where he could be of service to God in a church. On the advice of a former pastor, he enrolled as a ministerial student at Cumberland College with a major in Elementary Education for the first semester of the 1954-1955 school year and began classes in September.

Roy became a member of the Gospel Team that gave ministerial students and volunteers a chance to practice speaking and singing before a live congregation.

In January1955, on Wednesday before semester tests were to begin on Monday, Roy awoke with a very unusual pain in his side and an unusual stomach ache. From what he had heard about appendicitis, he thought that might be the problem; however, he did not say anything about this to his family and went on to the morning classes, one of them being a science class under Professor Hanes. During the noon break he went to his doctor. After examining

Roy, the doctor told him that he had acute appendicitis and would have to have an operation. At that time, Roy did not know that "acute" meant that it was a serious condition and thought the operation could be postponed until the end of the school year. His doctor told him that the operation needed to be done immediately. He sent him to the Baptist Hospital in Corbin to meet the surgeon, Dr. Baily, for another test. After he went by home to tell his parents about the situation, he stopped by a friend's house to drive the car back home from the hospital to take his parents and brothers to visit him. On the way to the hospital, they stopped by Rockhold High School to pick up his brother Jay.

After the surgeon did some blood work to determine the number of white blood cells, he confirmed that the operation was necessary. At that time, one had to spend a week in the hospital after an appendectomy. Therefore, Roy told the surgeon that he had semester tests on Monday. The doctor told him that he would be able to attend classes on Monday. The doctor taped his stomach much tighter than ordinary. On Sunday, he was dismissed from the hospital, and on Monday morning he was back in class taking a science test. After the class, he told the professor that he really didn't know which test that he would have that morning because he had to have an appendectomy the previous Wednesday after being in his class that morning. A few minutes after class, he overheard the professor tell someone in the office that one of his students said that he had his appendix taken out the previous Wednesday. Roy thought that the professor didn't believe him; however, Roy made it through the rest of the semester tests and the following semester.

During the summer of 1955, Roy and his brother went to Cincinnati and worked in the Western Auto Warehouse for the summer. They stayed in a boarding house in Avondale, a community in the northern part of Cincinnati. The lady that ran the boarding house was Italian and said that pizza really did not originate in Italy. But she did make very good tasting pizza. For the Fourth of July weekend they bought a big box of fireworks and took them home on a train, which in retrospect was really a dangerous thing to do. However, several in the community enjoyed seeing them.

In September, Roy went back to Cumberland College and stayed in Mahan Hall, His roommate was a distant cousin on his mother's side of the family. Roy's grandmother and the roommate's grandmother were sisters. Roy heard in April 2013, that his roommate had died of cancer soon after he retired from teaching in Ohio. When Roy was a sophomore in college, he was selected to be the gospel team director. That year the team was invited to participate in churches in Tennessee, Kentucky, Virginia and West Virginia.

Rena was a volunteer on the gospel team. Her church in High Splint, Kentucky wanted a team to come to their church. She had to talk to Roy about forming a team to go to her church. The conversation didn't stop there. They became more than team members. They began to see each other on a girlfriend/ boyfriend relationship which led him to propose before the end of the year. Rena accepted the proposal.

All went well until spring break when he went home with Brock, a member of the Gospel team who lived in West Virginia. A female student wanted to go with them to her home near Ashland Kentucky. As they were traveling from Louisa, Kentucky, toward Ashland during some very heavy rain, the car hit some gravel that had been washed onto the pavement on a curve near a small bridge. The automobile slid into a bridge that caused the door handle to hit Roy in the hip. When a porch light came on at a nearby house, the boys and girl walked to it and were invited into the house. As soon as they went into the living room, where Roy lay down on a couch. Someone in the house called an ambulance to take them to the Louisa, Kentucky, hospital where a doctor examined them and determined that they were able to leave the hospital.

Brock's father came to Louisa to take them to the girl's home and continue to Brock's home, but when Roy started to leave, he could not walk because his pelvic hurt so badly. The doctor then decided that Roy should wait until the next day when a radiologist would be there to examine him. Therefore, Brock's father took the girl and Barry on to their respective homes. When the radiologist examined Roy, the doctor found a double fractured pelvic bone. The doctor told Roy that he would have to lie on his back for at least a month. Brock's father returned and took him to their home where he spent the week lying on the couch. During that time, Roy made arrangements with a funeral home to send an ambulance to take him to his home near Williamsburg, Kentucky. When the ambulance arrived, it was a vehicle that was used as a hearse. There were no modern emergency transports with emergency equipment or emergency technicians as there are today. Many funeral homes used hearses as ambulances.

Because the semester was so close to being out, his professors would send his assignments by the Bible teacher and a girl's dorm mother, Rena, and other students.

When Roy went to his doctor in Williamsburg he put him on crutches for two more months. What a blessing it was, after a month in bed, to be able to ambulate to other places. He was able to return to college campus for a few hours on the last few days. While he was there, he met one of his class mates who was going to become a teacher. Roy witnessed to him to become a Christian, but he refused to accept Christ. He began teaching in Harlan County. That Christmas Roy went home for the holidays to be with his family. When he opened the paper one morning, the first article that he noticed was a report of an accident that the friend had been killed when his automobile had run off the road. The report stated that he had been drinking. Roy was able to go to the wake in the friend's home. Roy felt very badly for the situation for as far as he knew the friend went into eternity without Christ.

When it was time for graduation, the faculty decided that it would be better for someone to walk across the stage to receive Roy's diploma for him. Therefore, Rena walked across the stage to receive his diploma. Needless to say, Roy is forever thankful to God for a caring faculty and friends at Cumberland College.

As stated before, Roy had proposed to Rena and she accepted. They planned a wedding for December 1957, which would give her time to finish Cumberland College and begin her teaching career.

The summer of 1956 seemed to be a long hot summer because Roy could not do any physical labor with his broken pelvic bone still in the process of healing. There was an apple tree in the front yard where he would take an old quilt to lie on under the tree until the temperature became too uncomfortable, and he would have to move somewhere else. There was no air conditioner nor a fan to cool the house. The windows and doors were opened and there were tall maple trees around the house that helped keep the house a few degrees cooler than with no shade at all; however, the house had a tin roof and no insulation in the attic. The house was very uncomfortable at night when there was not a breeze to blow through the windows.

During that summer, Roy's close friend was going through a serious physical problem. Two or three years previously, she and her husband were in a terrible automobile accident and were in a hospital for several days. The injuries left her with problems that developed later. After a baby son was born to them, her husband left her and went to Michigan to find work. He would not send her any money to help support the baby. She took out a warrant for his arrest, but by the time law enforcement received the information and went to serve the warrant, he had moved.

The friend developed a problem with her back that required surgery, but she had no money to pay for the operation. Roy knew the pastor of the First Baptist Church in Williamsburg, and thought that he may know how to help her. Roy took her to see the pastor. The pastor advised her to go to Baptist hospital that no longer exists in Corbin, Kentucky. The hospital was supposed to have charity funds that might cover the surgery. When Roy took her to the hospital, the hospital administrator told her that those funds had been depleted. Roy does not know what arrangements she made with the Jellico, Tennessee, hospital where she was able to have the surgery without any anesthesia.

After Roy had recuperated enough that he was mobile without crutches, his friend, Claude, wanted Roy to go fishing with him. Claude borrowed his uncle's fishing boat that was anchored downriver from the Cumberland Falls on the Whitley County side. They took the boat across the river and went up river to where it was safe to get on shore on the Pulaski County side without being in danger from the falls. Once ashore, they went to the point of almost being under the falls. Huge fish could be seen swimming in the pool of water under the falls, but they would not bite any of the bait that was offered them. Even though they did not catch any fish, they enjoyed being out fishing. Claude married and the couple went to Indiana to work where he developed a kidney problem and died at a very young age.

In the middle of August, one of the neighbors asked Roy if he would help him hang tobacco. Roy had lain in the bed for a month and on crutches for two months. He certainly was not in any kind of shape to hang tobacco, but he was the neighbor's last resort, so he said that he would help him. As the day became hotter, Roy become more tired and was glad when lunch time came when he could rest for an hour. That afternoon, Roy didn't know how much longer he could keep working, but they were about finished when a pleasant surprise happened. Rena and her young nephew from Michigan came to see him. After a few more minutes of working the neighbor said that they were through and he could go on home. What a relief that was!

CHAPTER 6

R oy had majored in elementary education and received a temporary elementary teaching certificate which was good for two years before it had to be renewed with sixteen additional collage credits. In August 1956, Roy began to seek a teaching position by going to different school districts to apply for a position. On one occasion, his brother-in-law took him to Campton in Wolf County, but the superintendent stated that he didn't have any openings. Roy went to the superintendent of the local school board and he told Roy that he really had a surplus of teachers if the ones on leave returned for the school year. He told Roy that the superintendent in Newport, Kentucky, needed some teachers. After applying there, Roy was hired to teach a third grade class. While teaching in Newport, he lived with his sister in Cincinnati, Ohio, which was across the Ohio River from Newport.

This class was a challenging class especially for a first year teacher. Some of the children were old for the class. For an example, one student was originally from Tennessee and was thirteen years old. He was a bright young man, but because he had lived in the mountains, he just did not go to school when there was snow. Therefore, he got behind in his education.

The classroom had been a cafeteria in a partial basement. It seemed that Roy stayed cold from his legs to his feet that winter. As a result, he kept a sore throat with tonsillitis and had to go to a doctor several times.

Two students were half-brother and half-sister with different last names. Sometime during the school year the sister told Roy that their last names were supposed to be reversed which seemed odd to Roy. Many years later when Roy was volunteering as a prison chaplain, the boy, who was a grown man, had committed murder and was in the prison.

During the school year, Roy had to use two sipping straws to examine each student's head for lice. Occasionally, he would find nits which was a definite sign of lice and would have to send that student to the school nurse for further examination. The classes seemed to move from grade to grade as a class according to achievement. The achievement test the previous year ranked his class the thirteenth class out of thirteen in the school system. At the end of the year, they were ranked eighth out of the thirteen which was a great deal of progress for a rookie teacher.

During the school year, a new third grader from Michigan was placed in Roy's class. One day, he said that his mother was taking him to Michigan to see his grandmother. As the conversation continued, he told Roy the grandmother's name. Much to Roy's surprise, his grandmother was Roy's aunt on his father's side

The teaching salary was low, $2,400 for the school year, which was divided into twelve months. Then, after taxes and retirement fees, Roy drew a whopping sum of $150 dollars per month. In November, he took a part time night job as an orderly at a hospital in Cincinnati about three blocks from where he lived to be able to pay some bills that he had accumulated while in college. Also, this provided him with a summer job because he needed extra money. He would leave school and stop by where he lived for a few minutes then continued on to work. The part time working days were four days on and three days off. It became tiring at times. At the end of the shift at night, some of the orderlies would go to the cafeteria where the cooks had some of the best tasting soup that anyone would want to eat.

The schools were dismissed on Thursday afternoons during the month of October for teachers to visit the children's homes. Some of the children lived in a government housing project, while others were living in single homes, and still others lived in apartments. Roy visited in a third story apartment that looked like an attic. There were several steps missing from the stair casing. The flooring looked as if boards had been put down for the furniture to sit on. This was one of the worst physical homes that he visited. The home visits showed the parents that the teachers did care for the children. Also, the teachers would have a better understanding of some of the difficulties and problems that their students went through. There were no school lunches. Hence, there were hour long lunch periods that allowed the children to go home for lunch. The teachers could walk the two or three blocks to a restaurant for a hot lunch.

During November 1956, Roy received a notice from the draft board in Cincinnati where he had registered for the draft to report for a physical examination for the Army. He had Dr. Greenberg, who had performed the heart catheterization, to write a note concerning the heart condition. Also, he had Dr. Eversole, to write a note concerning the fractured pelvic bone. The note stated that he would not be able to do military duty for a year after the accident. He presented these notes to the examining doctor. Of course, he was given a 4F classification that meant he failed the physical examination. He thought that he would not be bothered again by being called up by the draft board, but little did he know what God had in store for him

That year Roy attended the largest church in the Cincinnati area, Lockland Baptist Church, with a friend that lived on the same street. This is where he first learned how to witness for the Lord. He believed that when he accepted Christ that God put that passion in his heart because he really wanted to see people accept Christ. This training has stayed with him ever since. In addition, he taught a young men's Sunday school class and participated in the church's Vacation Bible School that summer.

Toward the end of May 1957, he received another notice from the draft board to be reexamined for the Army in the middle of June. He thought that his records would have the notes concerning the heart and hip conditions, and he would not pass the physical examination. However, to his surprise, a few days after the examination he received a 1A classification which meant that he would be called into the Army.

In July, he thought that if he had only taught a few weeks and had to quit teaching to go into the military that the situation would not be fair to the school children to have to change teachers. He thought that if he volunteered that he would have to go in for four years which he did not want to do. When he called the draft board, he was told that if he volunteered for the draft that he would only have to serve two years. Therefore, he volunteered for the draft and was told that he would be drafted in August or September depending on how many volunteered for the Army. About two weeks later he began to think that if he passed the physical for the Army would the Air Force take him. When he called the Air Force Recruiting Office, he was told that he would be accepted if the draft notice had not been sent. He called the Draft Board and was told that the notice had been sent which came the next day. Looking back, he knew the Lord was working in his life.

When the draft notice came, it stated that he was to report for duty at. Ft. Thomas, Kentucky on August 8, 1957. The next couple of weeks he spent getting ready for two years in the Army. One of his brothers told him that he would not be able to take basic training, and after a Navy doctor had told him that he would never have to do military duty.

Roy had to give notice to the Newport Board of Education and the hospital that he would be resigning to go into the Army. He wanted to spend some time with family before he had to be gone for two years and did not know when he would be able to see them again. Also, he wanted to be with his fiancé before leaving for the military.

CHAPTER 7

On August 8, 1957, Roy reported to the induction center at Ft. Thomas, Kentucky for a life changing experience in the Army. After being inducted into the Army, he, along with about twenty other men, were given Greyhound Bus tickets from Cincinnati to Ft. Knox, Kentucky, where he would spend the first seven months of his Army career. First, there was The Reception Center where all of the personal data was taken. After a few days in The Reception Center, he along with other recruits were taken to their basic training company where they were to be transformed into soldiers in the best Army in the world, the United States Army.

The first week was Zero Week because that was the week he got his GI haircut, all the medical shots that were required, and the Army clothing that fit or did not fit at the time. At first, it was hard waking up every morning at 4:00 A.M. to a whistle and a shout of, "Rise and shine," and an hour of physical training before breakfast. He really didn't consider basic training too difficult having been raised on a farm where the work was hard and long hours were common. The training company was the last one for the company commander because he was being transferred to a different base. The drill sergeant was a different kind of person. He was left over from the Korean War. He probably did not have an education beyond the eighth grade and a very limited vocabulary. Roy believes on some weekends the sergeant spent his time in Louisville or Tennessee.

Labor Day weekend came after a week of training and the company had the weekend off. Roy had a thirty-six hour pass to go into Louisville, to see a college friend who was studying in the Southern Baptist Theological Seminary and was a Royal Ambassador Leader in a church. A thirty-six hour pass during basic training was almost an unheard of thing.

There were long hikes and learning how to fire the M1 rifle. Solders were required to be able to take the rifle apart and reassemble it in a very short time. Roy had no difficulty with that. Soldiers were required to make at least 160 points on the rifle range at qualifying time. Roy qualified with 165 points, but that was not good enough for the company commander. Roy had to go back to the rifle range to make a higher score. His buddy told him to take his rifle because he had a very high score, and said that it had already been adjusted for "Kentucky windage" Roy did his best on the rifle range but could only come up with 155 points which was not enough to pass the test. The first 165 points counted.

Another incident that was probably unusual in basic training was a mud fight. One day, when the company was in training on the field, a rain shower occurred and created mud. A couple of men started throwing mud balls at each other. Before long, several men divided into teams and had a mud fight. To the rest of the men it was amusing. The Commanding Officer said that the men were learning good battle strategy.

There were three notorious hills, Heart Break, Old Misery, and Agony that the trainees had to do double time up them with a full back pack. Roy can't remember which one it was, but he and three or four others ran out of energy and didn't reach the top as soon as the rest of the company. The company commander said that they would have to do extra physical exercise training when they returned to the barracks, but it didn't happen.

During training, the men who wanted to go to chapel services on Sunday went to hear the chaplain give his sermon. The chapel was very warm and some men fell asleep during the service. Time was spent in the dayroom or just idling around the barracks socializing. Also, one could do laundry or shine boots and slippers.

One day, Kevin, Roy's friend, who passed away at an early age, from his home community who was in basic training in a different company for either the National Guard or Army Reserves came to him and wanted to know if Roy wanted to go home with him that weekend. Roy told him that he couldn't get a weekend pass. The friend said he wouldn't need one because they would be back for count time on Monday morning, but Roy refused to go because he didn't want to get in trouble.

A few days before basic training was over, all the recruits received orders as to what their Military Occupation Specialist would be, and where they would go for their next school of training. When Roy read his orders, they stated that he was assigned to the Clerk

Typing School at Ft Knox. This meant that he would spend his time in the Army behind a desk in an office and not in the fields when the weather would be cold, snowing, or raining.

Between boot camp and Clerk Typing School, Roy had a ten day leave. He was able to spend a few days with his parents. Also, he was able to go to visit Rena in High Splint. They discussed what to do about wedding plans. They came to the conclusion that when he received his orders after Clerk Typing School, which would be in December, and if he would be stationed back in the states, that they would go ahead with the wedding. But if he were to be assigned overseas, they would wait until he came home to have the wedding.

Clerk Typing School went very well. Several of his basic training buddies were there. Because Roy had typing in high school he was put in the advance class with others who already knew how to type. The instructor reviewed some of the typing skills, but spent most of the time typing documents for the offices on the post.

One Saturday afternoon, Roy and some of his friends went to Mammoth Cave and the Floyd Collins Cave. Then, on Thanksgiving Day, One of his buddies who was a teacher as well as a spelunker and the ones who went to Mammoth Cave, went to a cave that the buddy knew about that was close to Corydon, Indiana. This trip was to explore the cave. It was fun but a little scary at times especially when some of them went down a rope to another level and had to climb back up the rope.

One day, when Roy was outside his barracks, he saw another trainee who was from the same area as he was and had gone to the same high school. He had a twin brother who did not have to go in the military.

When the orders came at the end of Clerk Typing School, Roy could hear some of the men say that they were going to Germany, others to different bases in the states. His buddy's orders were to France while Roy's orders were back to Ft. Knox to a replacement company. This meant that the wedding was on. Roy got in touch with Rena as soon as he could with the good news. They set the date for December 24, 1957, Christmas Eve, which was on Tuesday after graduating from Clerk Typing School on Thursday.

CHAPTER 8

Thursday after noon, December 19, 1957, Roy boarded a Greyhound bus for Louisville. In Louisville, he had to change busses to Lexington where he had to transfer to another bus for Corbin and then take a cab on to his home in Buffalo.

Early on Friday morning, Dr. Matthews, one of his college professors at Cumberland College, came to the house to tell Roy that Rena had called him and asked him to come and tell Roy that his blood work results had to be in the courthouse in Harlan by a certain time that day. Roy didn't dally any since he had to go to Dr. Eversole in Williamsburg to have the blood test done. He waited until the doctor could make out the report and drove on to Harlan, Kentucky While there, the clerk told him that it would take three working days before she could let Roy have the Marriage License, but since he was in the Army and didn't have that much time she would go ahead with the license on Tuesday. That was a relief. Also, she said that Rena's father would have to sign for Rena since she wasn't twenty-one. Then, Roy continued on to High Splint, Kentucky, to spend some time with Rena.

On Tuesday, the wedding day, Roy, his mom, and

brother drove back to Harlan for the big day. When Roy went to the clerk's office to get the Marriage license, it was closed. Needless to say, Roy was upset to think that he couldn't get the license. Roy went to the Sherriff's Office to investigate the reason. Someone in the office told him that because it was Christmas Eve the staff was having a party and would open up soon. Finally, a clerk opened the office. When she handed the license to Roy she told him that Rena's father had not signed the form and for him to come and sign it. Rena's father never did sign the document. After a few years of marriage, Roy teased Rena and asked her if she thought they were legally married. A quick reply was, "Yes."

The pianist started playing the wedding march before it was time and the minister had Jay, the best man, and Roy go with him to the altar. When Rena realized what was happening, she came in with the flower girls and her bride's maids.

In actuality, they were married before the time they were supposed to be married. Because of the way things happened, Roy knew that it was God's will that the two were meant for each other.

After the wedding reception in the church, Roy and Rena took his mom and Jay back home. From there, Rena and Roy went to Cumberland Falls DuPont Lodge where they spent their honeymoon night. They went to Cincinnati to visit his sister and her family before he reported back to Ft. Knox.

Rena had never eaten White Castle hamburgers but was introduced to them one night while staying with Helen. Roy's brother-in-law, worked the night shift for a printing company and often came in late or in the early morning hours. One night, about 2:00 A.M. he came in with a bag of White Castle Hamburgers and insisted that everyone get out of bed and eat them. Rena would tell about that experience every chance that she had the opportunity.

CHAPTER 9

R oy's new assignment was with a replacement company that was not a permanent assignment. While there, Roy was a clerk typist in Ft. Knox headquarters. About two weeks went by when Roy was reassigned to the Reception Center where he thought would be his permanent assignment.

The Reception Center was the place where the receptionists took personal information from the new recruits. The information consisted of family names, medical history and other details. The procedure was to have an entire group in the morning. In the afternoons, there was only one soldier who stayed to make corrections.

Rena had written Roy that the young man who had delivered the flowers to their wedding was coming to Ft. Knox. One morning, when going over the list of recruits, Roy saw the young man's name. When Roy went downstairs and asked for him, he was a little apprehensive because just coming into the Army and being singled out was enough to make one a little nervous. He was relieved when Roy told him that he had delivered flowers to his wedding just a few weeks before.

One afternoon, about three weeks later, when Roy was doing the corrections, he heard the phone ring and the sergeant answered it. After she hang up the phone, she came to Roy and said, "You have been put on overseas alert to Europe." This meant that Roy would not be staying at Ft. Knox. When he received the orders, they were for USAERHQ in Germany.

Before Roy left Ft. Knox, he had to get several shots. The female major who was in charge of the Reception Center volunteered to drive him to the dispensary for all the shots at one time. He doesn't know what they all were, but they left a bad taste in his mouth. He was given a ten day furlough before reporting to Ft. Dix, New Jersey, to be processed for departure to Germany. While on the bus to Louisville, Roy thought that this is the last time that he would be seeing this place. He had no idea that in less than eight years God would have him living in Valley Station, about twenty miles from Ft. Knox where he would be seeing the area many times.

CHAPTER 10

During the furlough, he took his bride to Cincinnati, Ohio, to spend some time with his family and Bride. Rena only had two or three days off from teaching during that time. While she was teaching, he had to dye his brown boots black because the Army was in a transition mode of changing uniforms from khaki uniforms to green ones and changing brown boots to black ones. Since Roy had been issued brown boots, he had to dye his brown boots to black and make them look like shiny new ones.

When time came for Roy to leave for Ft. Dix, his brother, Claude, took him to Williamsburg, Kentucky where he took a Greyhound bus to Knoxville, Tennessee. There he transferred to a bus bound for Washington, D.C. From there, Roy took a bus to Trenton, N.J. and on to Ft. Dix.

While in Ft. Dix, he and about five other soldiers were put on a detail to clean out a ditch on the golf course. The temperature was cold and the men needed to drink something warm. One of the men said that he would go to the clubhouse to get some coffee to help them keep warm. When he arrived at the clubhouse, an officer told him that he couldn't have any coffee. Then the men decided that if the officers thought that the men weren't good enough to have coffee that they weren't good enough to dig their ditch. So, they sat down until the sergeant came for them.

CHAPTER 11

After two weeks in Ft. Dix, the troops that were leaving for Europe had to board buses to make the trip to Brooklyn, N.Y. to board the troop ship, U.S.S. Upshur. While going through Brooklyn, Roy saw house after house that looked exactly alike. He thought to himself that if a person came home drunk and had forgotten his house number he would have a hard time finding the right one.

After boarding the ship, the troops were immediately directed to their quarters where there were bunks stretched like hammocks and stacked four high. Roy was fortunate to have the bottom bunk. Shortly after the ship was under way, the tugs guiding the ship out of the harbor turned the ship loose. The fire drill sounded for all the troops to go on deck. When the troops arrived on deck, they discovered the ship was passing The Statue of Liberty. That was a landmark that Roy had been wanting to see for a long time. They soon were told that they would be sailing along the Atlantic Coast to Savanna, Georgia, to pick up part of the Third Army Division that was going to Europe.

The voyage down the coast was rough because it was in the middle of March, and many of the soldiers became seasick. Tug boats met the ship at the mouth of the Savannah River for the Harbor Captain to guide the ship with aid of tugs up the river and into the port. When the ship came to the dock, one tug got on one end of one side of the ship and another tug was on the other side and end of the ship and turned the ship around in the Savannah to dock it. The soldiers were not allowed to go ashore. The next day about nine hundred soldiers boarded the ship for the voyage to Germany.

The voyage from Savannah to Bremerhaven, Germany took 9 days, and was an experience in itself. All the men were assigned some kind of duty on the ship and Roy's duty was to serve in the chow line at a certain time. Everyone had a certain time to eat their meals because altogether there were about eighteen hundred soldiers, some of their dependents, and the crew. During most of the meals, one hand had to hold the chow tray and the other one to eat with, or the tray would slide off the table onto the floor because of the rocking of the ship. On one occasion the weather was so bad, and the waves were so high, that no one was allowed on the deck.

Another instance someone supposedly stole a soldier's green uniform. All the soldiers except the sergeants were sent to the top deck and then sent one by one to their respective bunk where a sergeant was waiting to search the duffel bag for the uniform. When Roy removed his Bible which was close to the top of the bag, the sergeant began to talk to Roy about it and told Roy that his grandfather was a preacher. After a few minutes of conversation, the sergeant told Roy just to put the Bible back and go no further. To Roy, that was a witness for Christ. Also, they had chapel services on the ship as well as movies and snacks to purchase.

When they neared the English Channel, the ocean current became very rough. The ship seemed to pitch both up and down and sideways. Now, it was Roy's turn to get sea sick. While Roy was serving the food, he would have to go out in the stair well and use the "barf bag." After his stomach settled down, he would go back to the serving line. When the ship entered the channel a pilot guide came on board to guide the ship through the channel. While going through the channel, the famous White Cliffs of Dover could be seen. The cliffs are made up of chalk streaked with flint. The next day the ship arrived in Bremerhaven, Germany. The troops went from the ship to a waiting train to be transported to their final destination. They were assigned four to a sleeper compartment. The two long bench type seats made beds at night. Also, there were two beds that let down from near the top of the compartment.

The train journey was a very fascinating one. In the early morning, bedding to be aired out was put in the open windows could be seen. Also, clothes were hung on lines. The steam engine whistle had that sharp tone like one can hear in the movies. The wheels going over the joints of the rails made the clickety-click sound. Roy could tell when the train was going through the rail switches by the sound the wheels made.

CHAPTER 12

Finally, in the late morning the train arrived in Stuttgart, Germany. The men who were going to USARERHQ were met by a driver who took them to their new assignment. It was in a compound that reportedly dated back to the time when the Romans occupied the area. The group of new men were briefed on what was expected of them and how they were to conduct themselves when they were off post. They were encouraged to travel as much as possible and were given room assignments. There were four men to a room. Roy's room was on the third floor overlooking Bad Cannstatt, a suburb of Stuttgart, which was on the Neckar River. There was a long railroad bridge where Roy could see the trains crossing which he enjoyed watching.

One of his roommates was from Georgia. One night, while outside the compound, he had gotten drunk. While trying to get back to the compound, the young man broke his leg when he fell over the river bank and had to spend some time in the hospital. Not long after this, he announced that he was going to become a preacher.

One of the other men was on leave to Spain. When he returned from leave, he told about going to the Valley of the Fallen, which had just opened, and how long the traffic jams were getting in and out of the place. Little did Roy know that he would be visiting there. The third roommate was from Michigan. Not long after Roy arrived, the roommates began to rotate back to the states, and new roommates would take their place.

A few days after the one of the roommates left, Roy was called into an office as part of an investigation of a child being injured by an ink bottle. It seemed that a mother and her young son were walking on the sidewalk under the window of Roy's room when someone dropped, or threw an ink bottle out the window, and injured the child. The investigating officer wanted to know if he knew anything about the incident.

Roy told the investigating officer that he did not know who did it. Also, he told him that he was a teacher and that he helped children, not hurt them. Roy really did not know what happened or what became of the investigation; however, looking back in retrospect, he speculates that maybe when the man who was packing to rotate back to the states had a partially filled bottle of ink and did not want to pack it because it could be broken and damage his clothes. Not thinking that someone might be under the window, he pitched it out the window, and the bottle fell on the child.

Roy became an usher during the chapel services along with two of his buddies who already roomed together. When one of their roommates rotated to the states, they invited Roy to move in with them. After making arrangements with the First Sergeant, Roy made the move.

One of his buddies was from one of the eastern states and had worked for a communication company before coming into the Army. Another one in the room had worked for a well-known national Christian organization. Since everyone worked in different offices and could not talk about their jobs, Roy never knew exactly what the others did. Roy taught a boy's fifth grade Sunday school Class in the chapel program. A major was the director of the office where Roy was assigned. Roy had the major's son in his Sunday school class. One day, the major stopped Roy while working and told him that he wanted to talk to him about his son. Roy thought to himself this must be unusual for a major wanting to talk to a private about his son, but Roy thought that by this time the major knew that Roy was a teacher in civilian life. The major's son had gotten in some minor trouble and the major wanted to know what Roy thought about the situation.

The first week that Roy was in Bad Cannstatt, he was in the library and met a young man, Paul, from the southwestern part of the United States. Paul told Roy about a Youth for Christ service held in a German Baptist church in Stuttgart on a Sunday night. He and Roy began to go there about every Sunday night. The service was sponsored by Campus Crusade and a Minister who had been a missionary in Laurel County, Kentucky, was the director. The music director was a soldier from nearby military post. Several years later he became the director of the Southern Baptist Brotherhood in charge of the Royal Ambassadors.

Many Christian young people from different countries attended the service at various times. There were two young German men about seventeen years old who lived in Bad Canstatt and rode the same tram as Paul and Roy. Paul and Roy would invite them to go to the movies with them or to go bowling and to chapel. Since Roy has forgotten their names, he will call one Peter and one Jan. Jan invited Roy to go to church with him one Sunday. This was a great experience for him. Of course, the service was in German which Roy could not understand and did not know if it was a Catholic or Lutheran service, but he thinks it was Lutheran.

Peter's father was the director of parks. Jan's father was a doctor who had been in WW II and had been captured by the Russians. Also, he had a model HO scale train lay out which was very fascinating to Roy.

Jan told Roy that his father would like for him to have lunch with them on the opening day of the October Fest and watch the parade from their upstairs window. Roy felt it a blessing for him to be able to watch the parade from such an advantage point. After the parade, Jan's father took Jan, his mother and Roy for a drive in his Mercedes in the country side. While they were out, he stopped at a guesthouse for refreshments. Jan's mother asked Roy, "Have you ever been to the Kentucky Derby?" Roy told her that he had never attended the Derby.

After Roy returned home, he and Jan corresponded for some time, but during moving from one place to another, Roy lost Jan's address. Roy will always remember the friendship that was shown to him by Jan and his family while he was in Germany. This experience could be why the first exchange student Roy had was from Germany.

Paul and Roy became friends with a Master Sergeant who had at one time been a Major but had been demoted because of the downsizing of the military. On Saturdays and Sundays he liked to drive them through the country side and explore old churches and enjoy the scenery. The sergeant bought an old Grandfather Clock to ship home. Because it was too large to ship back to the United States, he sawed it into two parts and shipped it back like that. He said that he could put it back together when he returned home, but of course, it lost its value.

To Roy's surprise, he met a civilian lady, whose husband was in the Army, from Corbin, Kentucky who worked in one of the offices of the headquarters. She told him that she and her family had a radio program on the Corbin radio station, WCTT. Her father was a local pastor and they all sang during the program. Before going to Cincinnati, Roy had heard them many times.

On the fourth of July, a few solders decided to take a boat cruise on the Neckar River that runs past Stuttgart. The boat carried passengers up and down the river like a bus or train would go from city to city. The boat navigated through some locks and dams that were very interesting to Roy.

A couple of other men and Roy went to see a cemetery that was close by the barracks. Sometimes there were two or three people buried in the same grave which was the custom. After seeing many of the dates of deaths so close to one another, Roy came to the conclusion that they had perished during World War II. Later, someone told Roy that Stuttgart had really been hit hard with bombs that caused much damage and many deaths.

The rubble of bricks and other unusable material that was destroyed by the bombs were taken to a site outside of Stuttgart. It made such a huge pile that it was named Rubble Hill, and a cross was put on the top as a memorial to all those who died during the air raids.

The soldiers had to take turns doing guard duty in the guard shack at the entrance to the compound. One night, when Roy was on duty, a soldier came in after the midnight curfew. At the same time, a man who had been drinking came from the Service Club. When they met, the one from the club started arguing with the late comer and soon it became a fist fight. Needless to say, Roy had to call the Officer of the Day to come and take both of them to the guard office. Roy did not know what happened to them after the investigation because it was not long after this incident that Roy had an opportunity to transfer to France.

In October 1958, Roy had an opportunity of going to Berchtesgaden on a Rest and Recuperation Leave. This leave was generally called a Religious Retreat because Bible lessons were taught, and it was much like a religious seminar. The journey was made by train with a transfer in Munich.

While Roy was in Berchtesgaden, the group had an opportunity to experience several things that he was very happy that he got to enjoy. One thing that Roy saw was Hitler's Eagle's Nest. The group could not go to it because the road to it was closed for the winter; however, Roy did take a slide picture of it from where they were staying. They were able to go through some of Hitler's underground headquarters there on the mountainside above Berchtesgaden. Another interesting thing that the group did was to go through a salt mine at Obersalzburg. They rode a wagon through the mine while the guide explained the operation of the mine with all the statistics that go with a sightseeing tour.

On another day, they were taken to Salzburg, Austria where Roy visited several places that he had read about. One was the birthplace of Mozart, the great musician. Roy had studied about him in the Music Appreciation class in college. When Roy saw Mozart's piano in the room, he appreciated him more than ever. Also, he saw the convent and cemetery where some scenes of The Sound of Music was filmed before the movie was made. When the group crossed the courtyard, rain was pouring and was nothing like when the singing contest was being held in the movie.

A contest was held to see who knew the most about the Bible. No, Roy did not win that contest, but he did win the contest of who knew the least about the Bible. The questions in the contest were like: How many animals did Moses take into the ark? When was money first mentioned in the Bible, or of what disease did Sampson die?

The answers to the questions are: Moses did not take any animals into the ark, when a dove brought a green back to the ark, and Sampson died of fallen arches.

Roy had a great time meeting other people from different denominations while on the leave and was able to forget the work back at headquarters. He again felt greatly blessed of being able to experience places that he had only read about in books.

After Roy returned to Bad Cannstatt, Roy's friend told him that while he was gone that he had bought a car from a soldier who was returning home and wanted to take him for a ride. While they were riding around, he told Roy that the Personnel Office in which he was assigned had gotten a TWIX, which is like a military telegram, from the French Headquarters requesting someone with a 711 MOS, Military Occupation Specialist, to be sent to the headquarters near Orleans about 80 kilometers from Paris. Since that was Roy's MOS, and he had two years of French in college, he said something to the effect that he would like to go, but his friend told him that personnel had already decided who would go and told him the names.

On the following Monday morning, the major came through the office and asked some of the soldiers if they would like to go to France. Roy believed that since some of them had been slacking off in their work that they took that remark to mean, "Shape up or ship out." So, they told the major that they didn't want to go. When the major came to Roy, he knew what the major was talking about. Roy told him that he liked being in Germany, but he would like to go to France since he had two years of French in college. After some discussion Roy told him that he would go to France. The major said that this was not final. That afternoon he called another man and Roy into his office and informed them that they would be leaving the next Monday for France. The other soldier had not been asked if he had wanted to transfer. Therefore, this was a surprise for him.

That week was a busy one for Roy. Of course, he had to be processed out of headquarters which included returning certain items that had been assigned to him. The sergeant in charge of the office had his roommates and the men in the office to come to his house in Robinson Housing for a cookout lunch. While Roy was there the sergeant told him that the major came to him and asked him to try and talk Roy out of going to France, but he told the major that a man did his best work where he was happy. Roy thought that was a compliment to him.

A few days before leaving, Roy had to go to the train station to get the tickets from transportation. The clerk gave Roy a choice as to what class, what time, and if he wanted a sleeper. Of course. Roy wanted first class, a sleeper, and chose a train that would be leaving late and arriving in Paris in the morning.

On the evening before leaving Stuttgart, his roommates took him to a very nice restaurant in the main part of the city and treated him to a great meal.

CHAPTER 13

With orders in hand, the other soldier and Roy boarded the overnight train from Stuttgart to Paris, France. After the train was on the way, the conductor came through to collect their tickets and see the orders. He told them that if they would leave their orders with him to show the French Border Patrol that he would not have to wake them when they stopped at the border at Strasbourg. Being a train lover, Roy could hardly sleep. He was awake when the train stopped at the border, but he thought that the soldier who, was on the other side of the compartment, had no trouble going to sleep. Roy could hear the border guard and conductor coming through the coach checking the passengers' passports and /or visas. Also, Roy could hear the train crew checking the car journal boxes, the bearings on the axel that fits on the train, to see if there was enough lubricant in the boxes to prevent a "hot box". A hot box occurs when not enough lubricant is present to keep the bearings cool preventing them to become hot and malfunction. Roy assumed that a French crew took control of the train for the rest of the trip to Paris.

When Roy woke the next morning, the fog was so thick that he could hardly see the landscape outside the train until late morning. Roy thought that the train stopped at Nancy before arriving in Paris at the Gare de l'est (East train Station). Not only did they have to transfer to another train, but they had to transfer train stations. After getting off the train, Roy met a soldier that he knew from basic training. He was returning from being deployed in Lebanon. There was a military vehicle to transport them from Gare de l'est to Gare de Montorusse from which the trains going south departed

When the conductor on the train to Orleans took their tickets, he told them that they would be getting off the train at les Aubrais outside of Orleans He said that someone would meet them there. Sure enough, when they arrived at the station there was a driver from their new company to greet them and transport them to their new assignment which was housed in a small French Castle, Chateau de Touch. This was approximately 8 miles south of Orleans and close to the Loire River. The next day, they were briefed about the rules and regulations concerning their new assignments. The other soldier was assigned to an office in Orleans, and Roy was assigned to the personnel office at the chateau where he had to complete the Morning Report and type other documents.

The chateau was part of a large French farm. Part of it was a U. S. military golf course with the club house about one hundred fifty feet from the chateau. The chateau was a three story building with turrets on all four corners. Offices were on the first floor and living quarters were on the second and third floors. About four men were in each of the rooms on the second floor. Roy's room was on the third floor where the rooms were only large enough for one person. Roy was the only married man living in the chateau. The other married men with families lived in housing away from the chateau.

Because there weren't enough men to have a government mess hall, they were paid separate rations. The men had a club into which they paid for two French cooks to cook for them except the Saturday evening and Sunday meals. They could eat at the golf course club house or at a restaurant. Also, they could eat at the PX at COMZ Headquarters or at a café in Orleans. The Junior CQ (charge of quarters) would drive an auto into Orleans to take the men to the theater, PX, or chapel, or to meet a new soldier at the train station. There were other meeting places for the return to the chateau. One place was a café where one could eat a meal or refreshments before returning to the chateau.

The office in which Roy worked had been a milk stable that was heated with a Coleman heater. Sometime in the winter, the dampness in the office caused the duplicating paper to stick and the machine would not function properly. They had to store the duplicating paper closer to the heater. Since the morning report had to be typed letter perfect with not one strike over or any erasers and out by a certain time caused some frustration at times.

While Stationed in France, Roy attended chapel services that were led by Chaplain White. Roy taught a fifth grade boys' Sunday school class in the theater before the chapel services. Also, Roy attended a Baptist church outside of Orleans that was made up of military personnel and their families.

The results of the bombing during World War II could still be seen in Orleans. The Sainte-Croix Cathedral was heavily damaged. It looked as if no effort had been made to restore the cathedral. The cathedral was and still is associated with Joan of Arc. There was a large statue of Joan of Arc on a horse in the center of Orleans.

There was a Catholic church in Orleans that was heavily damaged during the war. According to locals there were some parishioners in the church when the bombing sirens sounded. The priest took the parishioners to the back of the church and began to pray. The bombs destroyed the main part of the church, but none of the praying people were injured. What a testament that is that God answers prayers!

One day, Roy received a letter from one of Rena's friends in Georgetown College where Rena went after one year of teaching. The friend wrote that Rena was in the hospital, had an appendectomy, and was not doing very well. One of the men offered to lend Roy the money to go home on an emergency leave, but by that time, Rena was already out of the hospital and on the road to recovery. About a week after Roy returned home in August, Rena received the degree of Bachelor of Arts in Education.

The men learned that Roy did not drink alcoholic beverages. One of them told him that they were going to get him drunk before he left France. Late one afternoon, one of the Christian sergeants called Roy to the dayroom to talk to him. He told Roy that he knew that the men liked to tease him about drinking, but they did have a lot of respect for him. This taught Roy the lesson that people do watch to see if you "walk the talk".

One morning, when the Chief Warrant Officer came into the office, he wanted to know if Roy would go into Orleans and take his wife to the Army hospital. She needed to go for a follow up examination from having surgery. The chief stated that he had so much work to do in the office that had to be done that day that he really didn't have the time to take her and would like for Roy to take her. After he gave Roy the directions to his apartment, he picked her up and took her to the hospital which was outside of Orleans.

In January 1959, Roy's best Army friend in France who was a Christian, invited Roy to go skiing with him to Mont Blanc, France. Neither one of them ever had on a pair of skis. They never got off the beginners' slope. On the last day, the friend was going rather fast downhill when he came to a large ditch at the end of the slope. In the process of stopping, he sprained his ankle very badly and was very sore for several days.

CHAPTER 14

I n April 1959, the friend wanted Roy to go to the Netherlands with him and another buddy for a weekend. On the way there, they went through the city of Rouen where Joan of Arc was burned at the stake. When they crossed the Rhine River, they took a ferry boat that carried many automobiles and looked like a small ocean going ship. Traveling along the coast, they saw the dikes that held the ocean water back from flooding the land. It was a strange sight when Roy looked toward the ocean and saw a ship on a higher level than he was. As they went through Hague, Netherlands, they saw the Peace Palace where the World Court is held. As this was the time when the Tulip Festival was held, they saw large fields with each one having its own color of tulip. Almost every car they saw had leis of tulips on them.

After reaching Amsterdam and spending the night in a hostel set up for young people, they spent the day touring Amsterdam. One tour was on a canal boat. The tour guide pointed out some interesting sights and buildings. One building was the narrowest house in Amsterdam. Another house was almost leaning on the one beside it.

Also, they went through the shipyard where ships were being repaired in the dry docks.

The friend and Roy visited one of the friend's brother's friend who was studying theology at a seminary or university in Amsterdam. That night they attended a Dutch Reformed Church because the friend's father was a pastor in Oregon of a Reformed Church and the friend wanted to experience a church service in the Netherlands. The congregation sang some songs that Roy thought he recognized. Instead of offering plates, the offering was taken up with a bag which was hanging from handles about a yard long. They saw the Queen's Palace which was a beautiful building.

After spending another night in Amsterdam, they started back to the château. On the way through the Netherlands, they saw many different kinds of windmills. Most of them were not working because electric pumps were being used to keep the water drained from the land. While going through Belgium, they saw the wine country. The topography was relatively flat when they saw a fortress. As they got closer, the road started going downhill and eventually came to a river. Along the river was a very beautiful village and above it was the walls of the fortress. This sight made for a very beautiful picture.

CHAPTER 15

In May 1959, the friend wanted Roy to go to Spain and Portugal with him. Part of the preparation for going was to obtain military gas coupons to obtain fuel especially in France and where they could be used in Spain. He took some five gallon cans to fill with petro, gasoline, for times when he could not find a service station that would take a coupon. They packed their pup tent to stay in camp sites when they could find one. Roy can only remember staying in two camp sites. One site was in an orange grove in Spain and another one was in Portugal. The site in Portugal was a very filthy place. The showers were open for all to see, and the toilet was like a slit in the floor which was very uncomfortable.

On the first day of the leave, they went through southern France and up the French side of the Pyrenees Mountains. Even though it was in May, the snow had not melted on the top of the mountain. Of course, they just had to stop and take pictures of them being in the snow. After crossing into Spain, they were stopped by a walking road patrol to check their passport. Although the mountains were very beautiful, the road was very treacherous. It was very narrow, and there were no guard rails to keep automobiles from going over the very high, steep mountain side.

While traveling through the mountains, they went through the country of Andorra which is a principality. Andorra lies between France to the north and Spain to the south. Because Andorra has no airport, one must travel through either France or Spain to get there. The capital of Andorra is Andorra la Vella that has an elevation of 3,356 feet which is the highest capital in Europe.

After leaving Andorra, The friend and Roy made their way through the mountains and onto the plains to Barcelona. Along the way, they saw some young men lying in a field by a stream of water. This scene reminded Roy of Psalms 23. "He maketh me to lie down by the still waters." (KJV)

There were many historical attractions in Barcelona. One was the statue of Columbus overlooking the Mediterranean Sea, and another one was an unfinished cathedral that was started in 1882 and according to a site on the internet will not be finished until 2026. At this writing a site on the internet showed that a great deal of work has been done on the cathedral.

The two traveled west to Zaragoza where they saw a church that had been a mosque but was converted to a Catholic church. They stopped at Zaragoza Air Force Base near Zaragoza where the friend saw one of his home buddies and refueled the car.

Between Zaragoza and Madrid, they stopped at the monument, the Valley of the Fallen, which is a Catholic church carved into the rocks. Directly above the church is a giant cross that stands on top of the dome of the basilica.

This is the place that Roy's roommate talked about where the traffic was so bad. Valley of the Fallen was built by a leader of Spain, to honor all those on both sides of the Spanish Civil War from 1936 to April 1, 1939, when Franco declared the end of the war. On the day that the friend and Roy were there, the fog was so heavy that only the bottom of the cross could be seen from the parking area and the entrance to the bascilla. However, a few days later they were passing two or three miles from there and could see the cross from that distance. According to the pamphlets at that time the cross measures 492 feet tall and is 154 feet from fingertip to fingertip. It is situated at a height of 5678 feet above sea level.

At one point, they passed where a road was being constructed. It seemed that the workers were only using picks and shovels to construct the road and wheelbarrows to carry the dirt to other places. As they traveled in the afternoons, they could see what looked like people under trees taking siestas. It seemed that restaurants did not begin to serve the evening meal until 8:00 P.M.

One evening, they went into a very nice hotel where some high ranking U. S. Army officers were. One of the officers told them that they must go to their room and change their clothes into suits and ties. Because they did not have that kind of clothes, they found another hotel without the officers. Neither one could speak Spanish, but Roy was able to get a room by speaking some French with a clerk who spoke some French.

There were many interesting sights to see in Madrid. The most memorable sight was the bull fights. There were three matadors, bull fighters, who took turns killing a bull. Each matador killed a total of three bulls. It was the custom for the killed bulls to be given to places like orphanages. The bull fights were a gory sight and could hardly be called a sport but rather a spectacle. The king had a royal seat that looked like it was almost in the center of the stands. When Roy and his friend went to see El Prado Museum, they were disappointed when they found that it was closed.

In 1959, Spain was over 99 percent Roman Catholic and did not permit protestant churches to have any signs advertising their churches. Therefore, it was impossible to locate a protestant church to attend on Sunday. While traveling through the rural country side, there would be sheep and goat herders tending their flocks. There were no fences and the auto would have to stop to let the herders get their sheep and goats across the road. Many times there would be young school age boys tending the herds. These scenes reminded Roy again of the story that he read in the reading book, *If I were Going*, at Buffalo. Toledo, Spain, was another interesting place that Roy and the friend visited. They toured the El Greco Museum where they saw many of his paintings. Some of the paintings were the Disciples of Christ. They could only see the magnificent Toledo Cathedral from the outside because long sleeves were required before one could enter the cathedral.

In Granada, the Alhambra was a very interesting place and was built when the Muslims had invaded Spain and built the palace with the beautiful gardens. There was a movie being made there at that time. There was an area that was used for a harem. Also, the tour guide led them to a dungeon where prisoners were kept. This reminded Roy of the conditions that the apostle Paul experienced when he was in prison.

Segovia was another beautiful city that the friend and Roy visited. The Segovia Castle has served many purposes. One purpose was the castle for Queen Isabelle and King Ferdinand who supported Columbus in sailing to find the new world. The castle sits on a huge rock that looks like a ship from the rear. There was an old Roman aqueduct that was still being used in May 1959, to carry water from a river about 15 miles away.

Roy and the friend visited many other cities and towns in Spain. After crossing what seemed like mountains or very high hills where there were wild poppy fields and other beautiful scenery, they came to a place where Malaga could be seen facing the Mediterranean Sea. Malaga is the birthplace of Picasso who was a very famous painter.

Roy and the friend decided to take a swim in the Mediterranean Sea. They went to the beach that had portable changing stalls, changed into bathing suits, and went swimming. The water was so cold that they did not stay very long in the sea. The time was only long enough for each one to say that he went swimming in the Mediterranean Sea.

The next stop was Gibraltar which is more than just a huge rock. Gibraltar is the southernmost part of the Iberian Peninsula at the entrance of the Mediterranean Sea. The people speak English because it is controlled by England. As they were crossing the narrow strip of land, where the runway for the airport was, a gate went down while a plane either took off or landed. Roy saw a television show that said that Gibraltar is listed as one of the most dangerous airports because the runway crosses over a four lane highway.

There is a saying, "Solid as the Rock of Gibraltar," but a native told them that the rock had huge cracks in it. He showed them a round hole that had been carved at an angle. He said that it was made to put gun powder and cannon balls in to be used like a cannon. The cannon balls could be shot into the Gibraltar Strait to destroy enemy ships. There is no city name for the address. It is just Gibraltar. After getting back on the mainland of Spain, they headed northwest for Portugal. Of course, going from one country to another required going through check points at the departure country and then again at the country of entry. Sometimes these were a quarter of a mile apart. Sometimes the border patrol would only look at their papers, but other times the border patrol would have them unload the luggage and go through it.

The first sight in Portugal that Roy saw was a grove of cork trees. It was early in spring, and the cork had not been stripped from the trees. The cork is the bark of the tree. It does grow back on the tree and can be stripped again after a certain length of time. After traveling some distance, rice paddies came into view. It seemed that the workers were setting the rice plants in water. After a certain period of time, the water would be drained to harvest the rice.

As the two were traveling, they passed two women with each one carrying what looked like a heaping laundry basket balanced on their heads. A short distance later as they approached a bridge, they could see several women doing their washing in the shallow part of a river. One can wonder what it would be like if a woman had to wash the laundry in a stream of water. That was May 1959.

The friend and Roy spent their first night in Portugal in a camping facility. The facility was the worst one that they encountered while on their leave. It was necessary to take a ferry across the Tagus River to get to the capital city of Lisbon.

Lisbon was a beautiful city facing the Tagus River just before it flows into the Atlantic Ocean. Lisbon is the largest city in Portugal and the most western capital city in Europe.

Roy and the friend went to a rocky beach where a man had just caught a small octopus. The octopus slipped out of the man's hands and went back into the water. They watched for several minutes while the man looked under several rocks to find the creature but never located it.

After more sightseeing, the two started northeast toward the Portugal and Spanish border. Outside of one village, they got behind a large crowd of people who were walking that took up the entire roadway. The group went about a half mile and began to turn onto another road. When they turned onto the road, pallbearers could be seen carrying a casket on their shoulders, and a cemetery came into view. Needless to say, that neither Roy nor the friend had seen a funeral procession like this one. The experience left them with a bit of sadness in their hearts knowing that someone had lost a loved one.

After they had traveled for some time, they entered a city that was having a large celebration. There was a very long parade with a religious theme to it and was about the time of the celebration of The Lady of Fatima.

The weather was very hot, and the auto had no air conditioning. The friend had some kind of canned meat that he wanted to heat. He put the can on the dashboard until the contents became hot.

As the day began to shorten, the two started looking for either a camp site or any other place to spend the night. It was not until after dark and some worry, that they found a hostel where they could spend the night. The next day, they made their way to the border near San Sebastian. From the plains down to the border was beautiful scenery, but the road was narrow and crooked. Before getting to the border, they went through Balboa in midafternoon and needed to stop to get something to drink. Because it was siesta time, everything seemed deserted except one place that seemed more like a bar, but they did have Coca Cola. After crossing the border back into France, they spent the night in Bordeaux before going back to Chateau de Touch.

CHAPTER 16

A few weeks later, Roy and the friend had a seventy-two hour pass to go to Brittney that is the most western part of France. They visited St. Malo which had been a notorious pirate haven at one time but became a tourist attraction. Next, they traveled to a western point of France where a lighthouse was located. The lighthouse keeper told them the history of the lighthouse and the distance that a ship could see light that was projected from the lighthouse.

Traveling along the road, crosses with flowers by them or statues of Mary could be seen by the roadside. The friend and Roy discussed the scenes and came to the conclusion that they were in memory of someone who was killed in an auto accident. A note of interest is that there are many crosses in the United States that are in memory of someone who has been killed in an auto crash. A scene of a village along the seacoast in a cove reminded Roy of a picture in *If I were Going.*

The return trip took them through a small town where they saw a woman throwing a pan of water from a second story window. Not very far from there, on each side of the street was a French lady who was wearing a very tall crochet white hat. The hat looked to be about 10 inches in diameter and about fifteen inches high. This was on a Sunday and probably was a part of the church dress.

They had to cross a river on a pontoon bridge that was down in a valley, but a high bridge was in the process of being built. The original bridge probably had been destroyed during World War II.

Another memorable incident occurred when a passing auto caused a rock to hit the windshield of the Renault, the automobile. The impact caused the windshield to crack into small pieces except for about a ten inch circle in front of the driver which was the safety part of the windshield. To keep the windshield from completely falling out, the friend stopped at an infirmary in a U. S. Army installation to get wide bandaging tape to put across the windshield. This did help keep the windshield from collapsing into the auto, but the friend could only see through that small part that was not shattered. Because he had to drive much slower than the speed limit, it was questionable whether they would return to the chateau on time. They just barely made it in time before being AWOL.

CHAPTER 17

As time drew near for Roy to return to the states, his replacement was assigned to his office. When Roy's orders came, they were for him to return by Military Air Transport System leaving Paris Orley Airport. Before he left France, he had to go to the hospital to have the separation exam. Later he was debriefed by an officer about what he could reveal and what he could not reveal about his assignment.

In the morning of July 21, 1959, before leaving the Field Detachment Service, Roy knew that he would be leaving within the hour for Paris to take a plane home. For reveille, he asked the sergeant to let him call the men to attention to tell them goodbye. Soon after dismissing the men, Roy was on his way to a staging point in Communication Zone Headquarters in Orleans for the bus ride to a hotel in Paris for the final leg to Ft. Dix, New Jersey.

After having their baggage weighed and checked for the flight, an Army bus took the group to the military terminal of Paris Orley Airport. After arriving at the airport, Roy and another soldier whom he had met earlier in the PX in Orleans were called to the check-in counter and were told that they would not be going on this flight because they had been bumped from the flight and would have to wait until the next day. After another night in Paris and going through the same procedure as the day before, Roy finally boarded a Military Air Transport Service plane that was a four engine propeller plane bound for McGuire Air Force Base, New Jersey. Roy was told that for safety reasons the seats were turned around, and the passengers were facing the rear of the plane. The plane stopped at a military base in the Azores for refueling. Although the passengers had been fed an evening meal on the plane, they had another meal while the plane was being serviced. Shortly after taking off, and the plane was on its way over the Atlantic Ocean, the pilot came on the intercom and announced that the original flight plans were to fly directly into McGuire Air Force Base, but there was a huge storm on that route, and they would be going into Gander Air Force Base in Newfoundland. The pilot invited the passengers who were interested in seeing what the cockpit looked like to come and see it. Roy who was seated directly behind the cockpit made his way toward the cockpit. As this was before the modern technology of GPS and many other technical advances, there was a flight engineer seated to the rear of the cockpit who kept up with the location of the plane and could tell the pilot what corrections needed to be made. As Roy passed the flight engineer, he paused to observe him. Roy saw him open a small opening to look through a porthole at the stars and look at the gauges. After doing some calculations, the flight engineer told Roy to tell the pilot to set his gauges to certain positions.

Since this was not a jet, the plane only flew at an altitude of about 18,000 feet.

The plane landed at Gander in the early morning hours of July 23, 1959. After deplaning, the passengers were ushered into a mess hall and fed an early morning breakfast while the plane was being serviced.

After a short time, the passengers boarded the plane again and made its last leg of the flight toward New Jersey. During the flight, Roy made his way to the flight deck and heard the pilot tell the co-pilot that when they arrived at McGuire that the air traffic controller would probably have the plane come in toward the east, and the sun would be in their eyes. As the plane got closer to the airport, the pilot announced that the airport was "fogged in" and that they would have to go into a holding pattern. It seemed like two hours before the fog cleared, and the plane was allowed to land after an eighteen hour trip.

After being away from America for almost eighteen months, it certainly felt great to put his feet on American soil. There was a sudden change in the climate for him. The weather climate in France and Germany had been much cooler than in Ft. Dix. The weather in New Jersey was so hot and humid that Roy had to take a towel to bed with him to keep the perspiration wiped off. One of the last days that Roy was there he was assigned K.P. duty, and one of the assignments was to help peel a bag of onions. Roy was very thankful when that last KP duty chore was finished.

Roy was surprised to see his good Army buddy from Germany who was there being processed out of the Army. One evening the buddy's brother came and took the two of them to his home for the evening meal. Meeting the buddy's family was a great experience for Roy. After Roy moved to Louisville, the buddy, his wife, and mother-in-law stopped by Louisville on their way to Florida to see him. While this roommate was stationed in Germany, he went to Sweden to see his grandmother for the first time, but when he arrived there, she had passed away, and he was only able to see her at the funeral.

On the way home from Ft. Dix, Roy traveled via an overnight train on the Pennsylvania Railroad from Trenton, New Jersey, to Cincinnati, Ohio. When Roy boarded the train in Trenton, he was wearing his Army uniform because that was a military requirement when he left Ft. Dix. Shortly after leaving the station, Roy went to the men's restroom and changed into civilian clothes. When the conductor came through the coach to take the tickets, he asked Roy where he boarded the train because he didn't remember him getting on the train, but when Roy told him that he was wearing his uniform, he said that he remembered him.

Shortly before midnight, Roy was standing in the vestibule when the train was getting close to Pittsburgh, Pennsylvania. The conductor came by and said, "If you want to see a beautiful sight stand out here as we come into Pittsburgh and see where the Allegheny and the Monongahela Rivers merges to form the Ohio River because it is lit up and is a beautiful sight." It was a very beautiful sight. He told Roy that he should be sure to be in his assigned coach before they came into Columbus, Ohio, because the train would be split, and that one section would go on to Chicago while the other section would go to Cincinnati. There was very little sleep that night. After the train left Columbus and came closer to Cincinnati, he began to see some familiar sights: Blanchester, Milford, Marie Mont, Norwood, and along Spring Grove Road.

After arriving at Union Station in Cincinnati, Roy went to his sister Helen's home. The next day, he drove her family's 1959 Buick to his parents' home in Kentucky where his bride was waiting for him. What a great reunion that was after being gone over seventeen months. He arrived home in time to see his bride, Rena, receive her Bachelor of Arts Degree from Georgetown College.

CHAPTER 18

Rena had already gone to Newport for an interview with the superintendent of Newport School System and had a teaching position for the 1959-60 school year. Roy had made arrangements with the school board to resume his teaching. Therefore, they stayed with Helen until they could find an apartment in Newport. After searching through the ads in the paper, they found a second floor apartment. The apartment had one large room for the living room. The kitchen was so small that one could hardly turn around in it and looked as if it had been a closet at one time. The bedroom was in what had been a sun room at one time and was very cold in the winter.

Roy taught a fifth grade class at Dora Cummings Elementary School. His principal, Miss Roberts, was a very easy going "old maid". Since Roy was the only male teacher in the building, all the other teachers looked after him, and he had a good group of children. One afternoon, Miss Roberts asked him to go to a principals' meeting for her with the Superintendent, Dr. Brown. Another time, a relative of one of Roy's students came to get the student to take him home because his father had committed suicide. There was a report of the father embezzling money from a union fund that led to suicide. Rena was assigned to Arnold School where Roy taught his first year. The same principal and most of the staff were still there. Roy and Rena's combined salaries were low and Roy had to sell his automobile for cash to help them make ends meet until they began to receive their pay checks. As time went on, Roy was able to purchase another car, a 1957 Plymouth. They lived close enough to the schools where they taught that they could walk to them and to the grocery store where they shopped. Also, Roy took a job at Christ Hospital to make ends meet.

Rena's brother, Earl, came to work in the area and found a job in Hamilton, Ohio. He stayed with them until he married his fiancé. It became necessary to find a bigger place and they moved into a larger apartment, but by this time they had bought an automobile and could drive to school. When they moved into the apartment, the landlady was an elderly lady and told them that she did not allow children. That was acceptable at that time because they did not have any children. About a year later, Rena became pregnant. Since a friend had an apartment available, they rented it. When Roy told the landlady that they were moving, she asked him why they were moving. Roy told her that they were expecting a baby, and she had told them that she didn't allow children. She replied, "I would have made an exception." But they moved anyway because Jim and Ruby Lamb, their new landlord and landlady, were two of their best friends and attended the same church. The apartment had larger rooms to accommodate the baby furniture.

While living in Newport, Kentucky, Roy's family attended Trinity Baptist Church which was only a block away from where they lived and made many friends. Also, Roy taught a Sunday school class in the Intermediate Department.

Before they moved, Roy received a letter from the Army stating that he had to do two weeks of reserve training and wanted to know in what year he wanted to do it. Roy wrote back that he wanted to do it in 1960. He received a reply wanting to know which two weeks that he wanted to choose. He chose the last week of May and the first week of June because he needed to find a job to work during the summer. Later, he received a letter telling him to report to Ft. Hayes in Columbus, Ohio. Columbus was about a two hour bus ride from Cincinnati, so he was able to come home for the Memorial Day weekend.

There was one event that Roy remembers very clearly while he was at Ft. Hayes.

One day, the commander was giving a major who had just arrived a tour of the facility. He overheard the captain ask a sergeant if he knew what some letters and numbers meant on the major's travel orders. He said that they had already called some other places including Wright Patterson Air Base and they did not know. When the sergeant did not know the answer, Roy asked to see the orders. When he saw the orders he said to the major, "You came here on a commercial airlines. The CIC letters are the abbreviation for Customer Identification Code and the numbers tell the accounting office from which account to pay the ticket." Roy was only a Private First Class which meant that he had only one promotion during his service time. A few minutes went by, and the captain returned to Roy and wanted to know how he knew that information. The captain had called some other places and inquired about the numbers and someone in authority had told him the same thing. When Roy told him that he was the morning report and orders clerk while he was stationed in France and had to know that information, the captain was surprised and said "So you are not a six monther." Roy told him that he had been drafted and was in for two years and had spent time in Germany and in France.

A "six monther" was someone who wanted to be in the Army Reserves or National Guards but had to take Basic Training and be on active duty for six months. The six monther was sort of looked down on by a career soldier, the draftees, and those who volunteered for four years.

After returning home from Ft. Hayes, he started looking for a summer job and found one selling insurance, but he didn't like that job very much, and it didn't last long. Then, Roy started selling World Book Encyclopedias. He did better at selling encyclopedias than insurance and won a trip to the Field Enterprise Office in Chicago for selling the most sets of books in a certain period of time.

Roy's Kentucky teaching certificate had expired because he had not been able to complete sixteen hours of college credits while in the Army. He contacted one of his former principals, Mr. Wells who had gone to Clermont County Ohio, to teach and sought his advice about teaching in Ohio. Mr. Wells took Roy to the county superintendent's office to see if there was a position open in the county. When they arrived in the superintendent's office, he said that the Batavia Elementary School principal had just called and said that he needed a teacher for the sixth grade. Roy believed that was the work of God because after interviewing for a position, he was hired as a sixth grade teacher. Roy taught on a temporary certificate and had to earn sixteen credit hours before the certificate could be renewed. By this time, Cumberland College had become a three year college, and Roy enrolled there to continue his education to earn a Bachelor of Arts degree with emphasis in education to earn a teacher's certificate in Elementary Education.

In the summer 1960, Roy's parents celebrated their fiftieth Wedding anniversary at his sister's home in, Ohio. Elmer was the only one who did not come to the celebration. After some of the family left, Greta, Roy's niece, was walking around the outside of the house when she fell and broke the end of her spine.

The baby was due in January of 1961. Rena taught up until a few days before Thanksgiving when she began to have problems and the doctor told her that she had to have bed rest. When the Newport Board of Education was told that she was expecting, the board did not know how to handle the situation because it had never happened before. The board decided to let her return to teaching after the baby was born.

At the same time Rena was having problems, Roy's mother became very ill with kidney and heart trouble and had been in a clinic but was home. He and his sister, Helen, went to see her during the Thanksgiving holidays. This would be the last time that they would see their mother alive. Then, on December 13, 1960, Roy's brother-in-law came to Batavia Elementary School and told him that his mother went home to be with the Lord. Rena was not able to travel to attend the funeral because of the distance of travel. His dad said that his mother had gotten up during the night to sit by the stove because she was hurting so badly. He said that he heard the coal bucket rattle, and when he went to see about her, she was lying on the couch and not moving.

On December 30, 1960, Roy was transporting some youngsters from Trinity Baptist Church to Silver Grove to play basketball in a church league when the auto hit a slick spot on the highway and hit a guard post. As a result, the front end of the car was badly damaged and had to be towed back to Newport. One of the other drivers stopped by the accident and took them on to Silver Grove. The next day when Roy arrived home from making arrangements to have the Plymouth repaired, Rena told him that she thought she needed to go to the hospital because she was having contractions. Therefore, she went into a local hospital in Northern Kentucky where Timmy Lynn was born one minute after midnight on January 1, 1961. He was the New Year's Baby for the Greater Cincinnati area. A local television reporter came to the hospital to take pictures and was featured on the 11.00 P.M. news. As a result, he received several gifts from various companies. Also, several salesmen came to the apartment. One of the men was a former student at Rockhold High School whom Roy knew when he attended there. Although the Lambs had been married for several years, they didn't have any Children. When Timmy was born, they treated him almost as if he belonged to them.

When Roy returned to school after the Christmas break, his school children were excited because they had seen him with his baby on television. While Roy's Plymouth was being repaired, his pastor loaned him his Corvair to use. When Timmy was a month old, Rena returned to teaching for the 1960-61 school year For the school year 1961-1962 school year, she transferred to Batavia where she taught a sixth grade class. After teaching only one year at Batavia. Rena decided to return to Newport to teach. She had some great students at Batavia, but she wanted to teach where she lived and be closer to Timmy even though he had a great baby sitter.

CHAPTER 19

Teaching in Batavia was filled with great experiences. The children wanted to learn. They came from a diverse background of parents: elected officials of Clermont County, bankers, doctors, newspaper owners, parents who worked in Cincinnati, owned auto dealerships, and farmers in the county.

One great experience was a field trip to the court house to hear a trial. One of the teachers who lived in the area inquired about a trial that the students could observe. A driver was suing a deputy sheriff for an injury that occurred when the deputy arrested him and was transporting him to jail. The deputy had an accident that caused the man to incur an injury.

The students saw the jury being impaneled and the attorneys began questioning the witnesses. When there was a request from the jury to see the scene of the accident, the judge ordered that transportation be provided. While the students were waiting for the jury to return, someone suggested that the students could take a tour of the local jail that was close to the court house. After going through the jail, it was time to walk the two blocks back to the school to have lunch.

When classes resumed, one of the students asked, "Was that acting or was it a real trial?" Roy assured him that it was a real trial. That student could dismantle a car and reassemble it. He dropped out of the eighth grade and started working. He came back to school and told the teachers how much he made which was more than the teachers were making.

One Monday morning, when the students came into the homeroom for roll call and announcements, they were very quiet. Roy sensed that something was bothering the students. He asked if there was something wrong or did something happen. The students replied that one of the students had been killed in a car accident on the previous Saturday. This came as a shock to him and had a great effect on the students. The reaction of the students showed that they cared about one another. On the day of the viewing, Roy and some of the other teachers went to the viewing of the body after school.

One of the physical education teachers planned a field trip for the junior high students to a place that required a great deal of walking. The students were required to have permission slips from their parents. When the day arrived for the outing, one of the students who was in Roy's home room did not have the permission slip wanted to go anyway, but her parents could not be reached by phone to get permission. Because she had been absent because of a sore foot, Roy thought it best if she did not go. The other teacher became a little upset with him and went to the principal who told him that the decision was up to Roy. Roy thought that if the child tripped on something and hurt herself worse, then the parents would blame him for letting her go and might bring a lawsuit against him and the Batavia Board of Education. Roy was relentless and said that she couldn't go. The other teacher seemed to not like that decision, but the next day her mother wrote a note to Roy thanking him for not letting her go.

In the afternoon of November 22, 1963, the office runner came into Roy's classroom and announced to the entire class that the President had been shot and killed. Of course, this was a shock to everyone. In observance of his death, school was dismissed until after the President was buried.

One day, in a science class, a student asked, "Since all the time zones cross at the North Pole, and if someone is standing on it, what time would it be?"

Roy said, "I don't know, but you could write to the Bureau of Standard Measurements and they might be able tell you. After a few days the student received a letter that read, "We don't know either, but we are sending your letter to the U. S. Naval Observatory and they might be able to tell you."

In a few days, he received a letter that said. "There is a circle around the North Pole that one can just pick out a time and go by it."

At the beginning of the 1963-1964 school year, Roy was told by his principal that one of his students had been diagnosed with a fatal disease and probably not live until the end of the school year. Every time that she was absent, he thought that this might be the end of her life. She lived until the middle of the next summer when she passed away. Roy was completing his work for his bachelor's degree and did not know about it until the beginning of the school year.

1964 was an election year for most of the elected officials in Clermont County. When it came close to election, Roy suggested to the junior high students, sixth, seventh and eighth graders, that they have a mock election. The students were very agreeable because some of their parents were running for election. One of the students said that her grandfather owned the newspaper and already had the sample ballots printed. The next day, she brought enough sample ballots for all the students in the junior high school to vote. At the end of the day, the votes were tallied to see who the students had elected.

The next morning, the principal called Roy and said, "Roy, I hear you had an election yesterday."

Roy said, "Yes, I did," all the time wondering if he had done something wrong and was in trouble for it.

The principal went on to say, "You had better bring the results to me because the candidates are calling to inquire about the results."

Roy thought that was an excellent experience and a lesson in citizenship for the students. One lesson was that their votes would matter when they became old enough to vote.

In December 1964, the Batavia school faculty was having a Christmas party at the elementary and junior high school's principal home. One of the teachers became very ill, and someone called one of the doctors in town. After the doctor examined the teacher, he said that he should be taken to Christ Hospital in Cincinnati which was about twenty-five miles away. He further stated that someone should call the hospital to make arrangements for a priest to meet them because he didn't expect the teacher to live because he was having a heart attack. Roy had worked in the hospital, so he made the call and told the night supervising nurse what the doctor had said. When the ambulance arrived at the hospital, a priest was waiting for it. The good news was that the teacher was alive, and after a stay in the hospital he went home, but he retired soon after that episode.

While Rena was home waiting for the birth of their second baby, she received several annoying phone calls that the person on the other end would hang up or ask for someone else. Roy reported the calls to the phone company and was told that the situation would be investigated. A few days later, the phone company returned the call and said that they had investigated the situation.

There was a saloon on the corner of the next block that had tapped into their phone line because they had discovered that no one was at home during the day when Rena was teaching. The phone was being used by a bookie to take bets. Rena was not bothered any more by unwanted phone calls.

Their daughter, Geneva, was born May 12, 1963, on Mother's Day, and was named after a teacher, Geneva, in Batavia who said that she should be called Geneva and that is what she has been called all of her life. A bakery on the next corner of the apartment gave a Mother's Day cake as a gift for Geneva.

CHAPTER 20

In August 1965, after Roy's fifth year of teaching in Batavia, Rena and Roy moved to Valley Station, Kentucky in Jefferson County where Louisville is located, to teach in the Louisville Public Schools. Also, Roy wanted to attend the Southern Baptist Theological Seminary.

Before moving, they had to make one trip to interview for the Louisville Public Schools. They met with the lady, who recommended the hiring of teachers, in a hotel where she took time out of another meeting for the interview. After being notified that both of them had been hired to teach for the 1965-1966 school year, they had to make two trips to find a place to live. During the first trip, Roy stopped at a service station and asked the attendant where would be a good place to live. He pointed on the map and said, "Stay out of this area." But the area where Rena and Roy looked, the apartments were much more expensive than they could afford. That trip was not very fruitful. But during the next trip, a realtor, who was a retired soldier, showed them a few houses including a house in an area where several houses were for sale. When Roy asked him why they were for sale, he said that the Ohio River had flooded the area the year before. That house was off the list. They finally settled on one in Valley Station. The owners of the house had built a new home in a different subdivision and decided to make their old house a rental house. One of the neighbors was a pharmacist and owned two drug stores.

After the moving truck was almost loaded, an insurance agent came and asked Roy if he had paid the last insurance premium. When Roy told him that he had, the agent wanted to see the receipt. That meant finding the box on the truck and getting the receipt out of the box. After the agent saw the receipt, he said that their agent had been pocketing the money and falsifying the records. Roy does not know what happened to that agent, but he probably was fired.

Early the next morning, while he drove the car, his friend drove the truck to Louisville. Besides the family, they had an aquarium that had to be oxygenated a couple of times between Newport and Louisville. After the furniture was in the home, the friend drove the truck back to Newport.

CHAPTER 21

After moving to Valley Station, Roy's family began to attend the New Salem Baptist Church located on Bethany Lane. New Salem was a small church and the members were very friendly. The pastor was a young man who was a student at the Southern Baptist Theological Seminary. While attending New Salem, Roy was ordained a deacon that was a blessing and honor for him. Also, he taught a class of fifth grade boys and a class of high school boys.

When the pastor resigned to go to another state, Roy served on a pastoral search committee. After interviewing some pastors the committee chose another seminary student. While he served the church, an educational building was built because the church grew spiritually and numerically. Unfortunately, after accepting another church in another state he developed cancer and went to be with the Lord.

Another position that Roy had at New Salem was Royal Ambassador Director (RAs). Royal Ambassadors was an organization under the Southern Baptist Brotherhood that provided early missionary training. One of the parents owned a farm in another county that had some caves and an old house on it. The boys loved for the leaders to take them camping there. They could learn about nature as well as doing Bible study and learning about missionaries around the world. One of the local high school basketball coaches who belonged to the Christian Athletic Association came and presented a lesson to them. He showed the youngsters that he could put a quarter through his ring. This really amazed the boys.

Also, Roy was the Training Union director for a year. That program was directed at teaching members the Southern Baptist Doctrine. Also, it taught about the missionary work around the world.

Rena was involved in the children's programs in Sunday school. She was a Girls Auxiliary leader that taught mostly about missionaries. This organization was under the leadership of the Southern Baptist Women's Missionary Union (WMU).

CHAPTER 22

Rena was assigned to teach in Semple Elementary School which was about two blocks from Churchill Downs. Roy was assigned to teach a sixth grade class at Jacob Elementary School on Wheeler Ave. Both Simple and Jacob schools were in the south end of the city. Since both schools were only several blocks apart, Roy would drive Rena to school and double back to his school.

One year, the theme of social studies was *The Changing Earth*. Near the end of the school year, an organization sponsored a train trip to Mammoth Cave. Roy thought that his students could see how the earth changes underground as well as on the surface. Also, most of the students had never ridden a train. The trip was on a Saturday, and some of the parents wanted to take the trip. When Roy called the organization to make the reservations, he was told that the train trip had been booked. That information was very disappointing to Roy. When Roy told the representative that he already had sold twenty-five seats, he said that he would call him back. When the representative called back, he said that seats were available. Roy supposes that another coach was put on the train, but the coach was not air conditioned and that made for an uncomfortable ride at times.

Roy, his wife, their two children, and a child from Spring Meadows Children's Home (no longer exists) in Louisville that they were sponsoring and had for the weekend, met the anxious children and parents at Union Station at 1000 West Broadway in Louisville. Riding the train over the Louisville and Nashville Railroad, that was chartered by the state in 1850, was a great experience for the children as well as the adults. Roy thinks that every student had to go to the water fountain and restroom at least two or three times.

When the train stopped in Cave City, Hart County school buses met the train to take the passengers on to Mammoth Cave. The cave tour was very educational for the children and adults. Without going into detail, here are some of the interesting stops and interesting places in the cave: Methodist Church, Giant's Coffin, Fat Man's Misery, and the Corkscrew. Today, the corkscrew has been replaced with a set of at least one hundred-twenty steps.

On the return trip, the train stopped for several minutes between two towns. Roy asked the conductor why the train had stopped. The conductor replied that the crew was checking to see if there was enough fuel to return to Louisville. He further said that if there was not enough fuel that they would have to call out an engine from Louisville to meet them and pull them the rest of the way to Louisville. Fortunately, there was enough fuel for the engine to return to Louisville.

During the summer of 1968, when Roy returned from a class at the Southern Baptist Seminary, Rena informed him that one of his siblings had called to tell him that his oldest brother, Elmer, had passed away in New Jersey where he lived. This came as a shock because Elmer's wife had not informed any of the family that he was ill. By the time that Roy knew that his brother had passed away from a stroke, he had been buried in New Jersey. Roy had not seen Elmer since August 1959. When he returned home from Europe, he went to Sears in Cincinnati to see him at his part time job. Elmer told Roy that his family would be moving to New Jersey because the company he worked for was moving there.

After Elmer and his first wife were divorced, he married another woman. They had two sons Willard and John. Roy had been to their home when they lived in Norwood, Ohio. He did not see Willard again until about 2005 when he visited Roy after visiting his half-sister in Western Kentucky.

Rena taught at Semple Elementary until October 1968, when she took a maternity leave because she was expecting their third child whom they named Letha. After Letha was born on January 5, 1969. Rena decided not to return to teaching. She became a stay-at-home mom, at least for a while.

Roy and Rena had decided to name the baby Nancy Eliza: Nancy after Rena's mother and Eliza after Roy's mother. Letha was born on a Saturday night, and when Roy took Geneva and Timmy to church the next day, the pastor asked Timmy what the baby's name was. Without hesitating, he replied, "Letha," so, that became her name. Timmy wanted her named after his baby sitter's granddaughter, Letha. The granddaughter's name was not Letha but Aletha, but was called Letha

About two years later, Rena became bored of staying home and decided to become a substitute teacher. She applied to the Louisville Board of Education to substitute and taught at Myzeek Elementary School in the city. In the meantime, she volunteered as a room mother at Johnstown Road Elementary School where Geneva was attending. When one of the teachers had to take a maternity leave, the principal asked Rena if she would take that position. She took the position and taught there until she received her Masters of Arts in Education degree with an emphasis in reading and moved to a federally funded reading program in another school.

To earn a master's degree in education, Roy enrolled in the Eastern Kentucky University. For most of the hours needed for the degree, he attended extended classes at Jeffersontown High School. Also, he had to attend classes on campus during the summer and commuted to night classes during the regular terms. On May 13, 1973, he received the Degree of Master of Arts in Education with emphasis in guidance and counseling. Although he never became a counselor, one of his professors told the class that a good teacher would do more good counseling than a school counselor would do because they had too much paper work to do.

In 1973, While Rena was teaching at Johnstown Road Elementary School, she began having trouble with her back. She had gone to one doctor, but he said that it was a pulled muscle. As time passed, the condition became worse. The pain bothered her so much one night that she couldn't sleep. She got out of the bed and sat in a tub of hot water two or three times. The next morning, as she was getting ready for school, Roy asked, "Are you going to school?"

She replied, "Yes, tonight is open house and I should be there."

Disgustingly, Roy said, "That is all the more reason you shouldn't go because you will be standing on your feet all that time." As Rena was getting out of the car at the school, Roy said, "If you need to go to the doctor, have someone take you."

About ten o'clock, Roy's principal called Roy on the house phone and told him that he needed to call Rena's doctor. When Roy called the doctor, he told him that Rena had come to see him and he sent her to a local hospital. After Roy's principal arranged for him to leave, he went to the hospital. Dr. Roberts had already admitted her to the hospital for further tests. The X-ray showed a herniated disc that needed surgery.

The Surgery went well. Dr. Roberts told her how long she would have to lie on her back and on which day she could sit up. When the nurse went in her room on the morning that the doctor told her she could sit up, she was surprised to see Rena sitting on the bed. The nurse asked her who told her that she could get up. She replied that the doctor told her that she could sit up on the third day, and this was the third day. The nurse told her that she should have waited until one of the staff could help her. She recuperated very well, and hardly ever complained about her back hurting.

On Monday, before Memorial Day in 1978, Rena was riding to school with one of her friends. They left about twenty minutes before Roy left to go to his school. When

he turned onto east Pages Lane, he saw a line of traffic
that was backed up from behind a school bus. Then he
saw a garbage truck turn onto a street and thought that the
garbage truck was backing up the traffic. When he saw
the school bus go around an emergency vehicle, he could
see the technicians were bringing someone on a stretcher
from a wrecked auto. He recognized the new blouse that
Rena was wearing when one of the technicians moved to
one side. When Roy stopped the car and started toward
her, he saw that one of the policemen was one who lived
around the corner from him. Another policeman told Roy
that he couldn't come to her. But when that policeman
was told by Roy's friend that she was Roy's wife, he let
Roy go on to see her and to find out what had happened.

She said that the driver asked her to remove a spider
from her breast area and when the driver looked down
that she went off the curve on the road and ran into a
tree. Rena hit her head on the windshield and her arm
was badly lacerated. The driver had a few bruises and
her eye glasses were broken. Both of them were taken to
Southwest Hospital which was about three minutes from
the scene of the accident.

When the nurse started to remove the blouse, Rena
told her not to cut it because it was a new blouse. When
the nurse took the blouse off her, a piece of her arm was
left in it, and came out when it was opened to be washed.
Needless to say, that the blouse was discarded.

The X-rays showed that three neck vertebras were
fractured. The staff called Dr. Roberts, the neurosurgeon,
who had her transferred to the same hospital where she
had the back surgery where he could take better care of

her. Dr. Roberts told Roy that if the impact had been any harder that it would have killed Rena. She was put into the Intensive Care Unit (ICU). The doctor put her on a Stryker Frame that could be turned so that Rena would be on her back sometimes and on her stomach part of the time. Also, he put Vicki Tongs on her head with weights to help the bones to grow back in a more normal position.

While Rena was in the ICU, the nurses would have Roy hold the weights while they turned her on the Stryker Frame or raise her body toward the head of the frame. After a few days in the Intensive Care Unit, Rena was moved to the fourth floor of the hospital. On Saturday night of Memorial Day weekend, a nurse came into the room and had Roy to leave the room while she attended to Rena. While Roy was out of the room, the nurse was turning Rena by herself and the Vicki Tongs came loose. Because of the holiday weekend, the doctor did not answer his phone for a long time. When he did answer it, he said that the tongs should be left off her head. As a result, her neck did not grow back normally and gave her problems the rest of her life. Neighbors would bring food to the house and that helped Roy visit with Rena for longer periods of time with her at the hospital. When one lady brought food, she said, "Do you know that you have a swarm of bees on the tree in your front yard?"

Roy replied that he didn't know and went outside to see for himself. Sure enough, there was a swarm of bees very low on a small cedar tree. He knew a man who was a bee keeper and had him to come and get the bees.

Rena was dismissed on the second day of July. That was a big relief for the entire family. She had to have help in eating and other activities because of the injured arm, Roy was not able to leave her for any length of time. She was able to pick out bits of tree bark that had remained in her arm around the area where it was injured. She had to do therapy on her arm for several weeks. Her goal was to be ready for school when it started in August.

While Roy was staying home with Rena on Wednesday nights, Letha began to go to Valley View Baptist Church to Girls Auxiliary. As time went by, Roy could take her to the church and stay during the time that she was in the meeting. After Rena was able to go to Church, she, Geneva, and Roy moved their membership to the Valley View Baptist Church.

When Roy taught in the Youth Department at Valley View Baptist Church, he and another person would go visiting some of their students at least once a week. When one of them had never accepted Christ, they would witness to that young person. On one occasion, Roy witnessed to a tenth grader in his Sunday school class who accepted Christ. Several years later, while Roy was grading his middle school class' papers, the phone rang. When Roy answered the phone, the voice on the other end said, "Before I tell you who I am, I want to thank you for coming by my house and leading me to the Lord. I don't know what I would have done without Him these last few years." He went on to say that his baby had been born with something that did not let the baby live but only a few hours. It was very emotional for him but it was the grace of God that he was getting through the loss of his baby.

CHAPTER 23

Roy taught many very wonderful children who went on to make successful lives. Some went into the medical field as nurses and X-ray technicians. One student who did have some problems and did not finish high school started his own company and became very successful. Later he told Roy. "You are the only teacher that I really liked because you are the only one that helped me." Of course, that made Roy feel good. However, Roy thinks that there were other teachers who cared for him.

After one of Roy's sixth grade students was in class for a long period of time began to get edgy and tense, he would begin to yell out in class and disrupt it. One day, he started to throw a chair at Roy. The student finally calmed down enough that Roy could take him to the office. Roy said to the principal, "This child can only stand to stay in class for so long, and then he becomes agitated for having to sit for so long. Is there any way that we can call his mother and let him come home when he can't stand school any longer because he only lives on the next block?" The principal called his mother and she agreed to the idea. He finished out the rest of the year at Jacob. The next school year the student was in the junior high school. Sometimes when he would get in trouble and would be sent home, he would stop by Roy's class and talk with him for a few minutes.

In 1974, Jennifer called Roy and told him that their sister, Alice, was seriously ill with kidney problems in Christ Hospital in Cincinnati. Since Alice had blood type AB negative, which none of the other members of the family had, finding a kidney donor was very difficult. She was put on dialysis while waiting for a potential kidney donor. She was well enough that she attended a family reunion in the summer of 1975 at the family's home in Walden. Soon after that she received a kidney transplant that seemed to be a success. Not long after the transplant, she had a bad rash. The doctor thought her body was rejecting the kidney, so he removed the kidney. When the kidney was examined, it was found to have been a chicken pox virus. The doctor thought that the virus came with the kidney from an eight year old boy who had been killed in a traffic accident in the Cincinnati area. Roy heard that the kidney had grown to almost an adult size in a very short time. On October 9, 1975, Alice was at home when she had a stroke and went home to be with the Lord at the age of fifty-two. Her funeral was held in Mt. Vernon, Kentucky and she was interred in a cemetery on top of a hill above Livingston in Rockcastle County.

About 1975, the Louisville Public School Board hired a new superintendent. He brought into the system a program called Focus and Impact to increase the test scores of the many schools that were far below the average. To teach in the Focus and Impact schools, a teacher had to apply to teach in those schools because the staffs in those schools had been declared vacant. The teachers had to take special sensitivity training that followed the psychology of Carl Rogers in his book, *I'M OK__ YOURE OK*. The federal government granted the school board extra money to run the program. The system went broke and had to let the Jefferson County Public Schools take control of the Louisville Public Schools. As a result, the two systems became one which was the Jefferson County Public Schools.

The Jefferson County Board of Education decided to institute middle schools which would include the sixth, seventh, and eighth grades. When this happened, Roy moved to Iroquois Middle School where he taught for the next twelve years. Then, he transferred to Stuart Middle School for four years. After spending thirty-five years teaching grades three through eight, he retired from the classroom. He continued to teach several more years in the Adult Education Program. All together he spent fifty-three years in education.

On March 22, 1980, Timmy married his high school sweetheart, Letha. They have a son Jackson. Jackson and his wife, Cindy, were married on October 10. 2010, and have a daughter who was born in March 2014, and a son born in August 2016.

On September 20, 1980, Jennifer called Roy to tell him that their sister Helen had passed away the night before from a massive heart attack. Helen had worked that day at a store in downtown Cincinnati. When Brian, her husband, picked her up after work he asked her if she wanted to go to her favorite restaurant to eat. She told him that she wasn't feeling well and wanted to go home.

When they arrived home, she practically fell across the bed. Brian called for an ambulance, but apparently she died by the time the ambulance arrived at the hospital or soon thereafter. She was interred in the Spring Grove Cemetery in Cincinnati. The cemetery is known as the second largest in the United States. It attracts school field trips to observe the many large artistic statues as grave markers and the arboretum. Later, Brian and his second wife were interred next to Helen.

After graduating from high school in 1981, Geneva went to Eastern Kentucky University to major in education and to play in the college band. She roomed with Clara who was one of her best friends from her home town. Clara was dating a young man, Samuel, who was going to the University of Kentucky had a roommate, Stanley, from northern Kentucky. Clara introduced Geneva to Stanley. As a result Stanley and Geneva became engaged.

When Geneva brought Stanley to meet her parents, Roy asked him if he had ever accepted Christ as his savior, he said that he had not. He said that he wanted to do that when he went to church with his grandmother in northern Kentucky. After a period of time, he came with her again. When Roy approached him about accepting Christ, Stanley said that he had not gone to church with his grandmother. However, he did let Roy lead him in a prayer to accept Christ. Geneva and Stanley were married on September 22, 1984, at Valley View Baptist Church. After the wedding they moved to Waco, Texas, where he already had a job with International Harvest. After a short time in Waco, they moved to Columbus, Indiana. Then, they moved to Northern Kentucky.

Geneva had a set of twins, Joseph and James and fifteen months later had another baby, Caleb. Joseph has a daughter and James has a son.

CHAPTER 24

In 1985, at the encouragement of Geneva, Rena and Roy decided to sponsor a foreign exchange student for the school year. They found an ad in the local paper seeking a host family. When they contacted the Foreign Exchange Student Representative, she sent them an application form which they completed. After the representative reviewed the application, she visited Rena and Roy's home to determine if they were suitable for the student and gave them a copy of the student's application.

On the application was a question, Would you go to church with your host family? He wrote I would go for the social aspect. The first Sunday that John, the student, went to church with Roy's family, the pastor's sermon title was "When Fools go to Church." On the way back home, Rena asked John what he thought about the sermon. He replied that the pastor didn't have any right to say the things that he said. Rena reminded him that it was the Bible.

The first week that John was here, he went with the youth group at Valley View Baptist Church to Kings Island in Ohio and made some Christian friends. As time passed, he and Roy would have conversations about God and ways they could know that there is a God. He kept going to church and Sunday school becoming a member in the senior class, and joined the youth choir. Also, he wanted to learn to drive. After a few weeks Roy and John were out one Sunday afternoon, with Roy giving John a driving lesson, when John said that he needed to get back in time for youth choir practice. That night during church, John was sitting with some of the youth, while Roy was sitting on one end of a pew by himself. While a hymn was being sung, John came and sat beside Roy. Then he said, "Roy, I have to ask you a question, and it is hard for me to do that."

Roy replied, "What is it John?"

He said, "I want to know how to be saved?"

That just about blew Roy away, but it really thrilled him at the same time. He thought that this might take some time. So, he decided instead of going to the altar because this might cause a distraction from the sermon, they needed to go to a more private place. They went to a room where they could converse without interrupting the service. As they left the auditorium, Roy invited one of John's Christian friends to come with them. After they arrived in the room, another one of John's friend stopped by.

After Roy read John 3:16 KJV to him, John said that he didn't know what everlasting meant. Roy asked him if he knew what eternal meant. He said that he didn't. Roy just prayed to himself Lord, help me. Roy realized that John was a good student in math, so, Roy asked him if he knew what infinite meant and he told Roy that he did.

Roy explained that is what everlasting meant. After more discussion, John prayed for salvation and accepted Christ as his Savior.

John told Roy that he couldn't get baptized. He said if he decided to marry a German Catholic girl that his being baptized would be a problem. But a week before he returned to Germany, he was baptized.

Later, he came for a visit on Thanksgiving Day and asked if he could say the prayer. What a blessing! John went on to study at a northern university Medical School where his father taught and eventually became a cardiovascular anesthesiologist in a southern state, where Letha and Roy visited him in April 2012.

During the summer of 1986, an Exchange of Foreign Students representative called Roy. She told him that Rena and his name had been given to her by their pastor's wife. The representative wanted to know if they would be interested in keeping a foreign exchange student from Sweden for a school year. The student had requested on his application that he would like to be placed with a Baptist family. After looking over Phillip's application, Roy and Rena decided to keep him for the school year.

The day before school began, Phillip said that he wanted to get up 15 minutes earlier than it took him to get ready for school because he wanted to have time to read his Bible and pray. Phillip went to Doss High School, where he made many friends. Also, he joined the Pepsi Singers. His picture was on one of the months of the school calendar.

Being late for going somewhere was his only fault. One time, he was told to be ready at a certain time to go somewhere with the family. A few minutes after time to go, Roy, Rena, and Letha drove around the block. When they returned home, Phillip was outside waiting and was never late again. Even today, many people at church remembers Phillip because of his outgoing personality. Phillip's parents and brother came to visit him while he was with Roy and Rena. His parents and brother visited New Orleans, where the music left an impression on them, especially his father.

For the 1987–1988 school year, Roy and Rena had decided not to keep another foreign exchange student. In January1988, a foreign exchange representative called them and asked them if they would keep an exchange student who was having to change host homes. After discussing the reason for the situation, the representative agreed to bring the student, Glenn, to their home to meet him. After talking to him about the situation in his present home, Roy and Rena agreed to keep him on a trial basis. The trial lasted until the end of the school year.

Glenn went to church and Sunday school with Roy and Rena. Also, he went to the Wednesday night youth services while Roy went to the adult services. One night, after Glenn was late coming from his meeting, he said that he did something that he thought that he would never do. When Roy asked him what he did, he replied, "I accepted Christ." He said that the youth had put on a skit that portrayed someone going to Heaven. Glenn attended Doss High School while he was in Louisville.

One of the students at Doss told Roy, "I didn't know that he was from a foreign country because he didn't have an accent." Glenn already spoke four different languages when he came to America. Glenn went with Rena and Roy to visit their daughter, Letha. Glenn asked, "Roy, how many states will we be going through and how long it will take?" When Roy said that they would be going through four states and take about fourteen hours, Glenn said, "If you drove that length of time in Europe you would go through that many countries."

About two years after Glenn returned home, he and his sister came for a visit with Roy and Rena and to see some American friends. Now, he is married and has a teenage son. He is now employed by a travel agent and has worked in Israel. He said that while in Israel he taught Bible lessons from the Bible that Roy had given him.

While Glenn was here, he and a friend from Sweden who was staying with a Foreign Study Educational Foundation representative, picked Christian from Sweden for Rena and Roy to keep for the school year 1988-1989.

While visiting in Sweden, Rena and Roy had an opportunity to visit Christian and his parents in their home. Christian attended Doss High School and church where he met friends in the neighborhood. In November, Christian accompanied Rena and Roy to Denver, Colorado, where Rena was a presenter at a middle school conference. Christian met a young man in the hotel who was a skier and went skiing with him for a couple of days.

One Sunday morning, Valley View Baptist Church had a guest singing group that Christian attended. Toward the end of the program, the leader of the group gave an opportunity for anyone to pray to accept Christ into their life. After the service, Christian told Roy that he prayed that prayer. Later, Christian said to Roy, "I wish that I had the faith that you have." Roy replied, "Christian, I have been at this for a very long time. I have had time to grow in the faith."

While Christian was here, his parents visited him in May during the Derby Festival. The weather was so cold that it snowed on Friday before the Derby on Saturday. Christian's father was a golfer and he had Roy take him to a sporting goods store where he purchased a set of golf clubs to have them shipped to his home in Sweden. Christian and a friend returned for a visit about three years later. They had bought an automobile in New York and was driving it to California where they were going to sell it before returning home.

When Rena and Roy were visiting Phillip in Sweden, they told his parents that if Phillip's brother, Albert, wanted to come for a year that they would keep him, and he would not have to go through the student exchange program. In August 1991, Albert came for the school year. Before Albert came, Roy inquired about the school situation. He was told that because Albert did not come through the exchange program that he would have to pay tuition, which was several hundred dollars, but if Roy became his legal guardian, he would not have to pay the tuition. Before school began, Roy took Albert and a letter from his father stating that Roy could be his legal guardian to the court. The judge let Roy be Albert's legal guardian and he did not have to pay tuition for coming to school from out of the country. Because Albert was 6 feet 10 ¾ inches tall, almost everyone thought that he ought to play basketball, but he had no interest in basketball. During Christmas break two of Albert's friends came from Sweden and took him with them to the Southwest of the United States. For several days. They enjoyed the celebration of Christmas at Roy's home. Albert made friends with some of the young people in church who would visit him. Roy took Albert to Washington, D.C. on a Saturday with a school group from Jefferson County Public Schools that had a special airline rate. After the group arrived in Washington, Roy and Albert left the group to go where they wanted to visit without all the noise from the school children. At the end of the day, the two met the group at the Washington, D. C. airport for the return flight home. Albert is now married and has children. Recently, Albert and Roy communicated on Facebook and on the telephone.

The last exchange student that Rena and Roy had was for the school year 1991 -1992 school year when Luke from Cologne, Germany, who came through Foreign Study Educational Foundation. Luke made several friends while he was with Rena and Roy. He went with Roy to visit Roy's daughter in the Northeast. Four years later, Roy was resting in a swing in his backyard. He saw someone come through the gate with a bouquet of flowers. He thought to himself that young man looked familiar. When the young man came closer, Roy realized that it was Luke and the flowers were for Rena. Roy does not know anything about him at the present time.

CHAPTER 25

In the spring of 1988, Rena and Roy decided that they would like to visit Europe. After discussing the places that they wanted to see, Roy called a friend, Lori, who was a travel agent. He told her where they wanted to go, in what order and time they wanted to spend in each place. Lori made all the arrangements for the trip and was only about three weeks after Glenn returned home to Denmark.

The first place that Rena and Roy wanted to go was Denmark to visit Glenn and his family. On the day of departure, it had not rained for 31 days. While waiting for the plane to leave, a very heavy thunderstorm came. After several minutes went by, the flight crew allowed the passengers to board the plane for Atlanta, Georgia. The plane sat at the gate several more minutes before it was backed from the terminal and went to the end of the runway for departure. After the plane sat at the end of the runway for several minutes, the pilot shut off the engines and said that there was a delay in departure because of weather conditions between Louisville and Atlanta. While the plane was on the ground, the flight attendants began to serve refreshments. After several more minutes, the plane took off for Atlanta while it was still raining. After the plane reached cruising altitude, the turbulence caused the plane to be very shaky, and the fasten seatbelt sign was on constantly. As the plane reached Atlanta, the pilot had to go into a holding pattern for several more minutes. By this time, Roy began to wonder if the plane would make it to Atlanta in time for the overnight flight to Frankfort, Germany, which was the first leg of the flight to Copenhagen, Denmark. When the plane landed in Atlanta, it was time for the departure of the plane to Germany. As the passengers deplaned at the terminal, an attendant announced that all the passengers for the plane to Germany to stand close by because they would be bused to their plane. When the passengers went into the departure terminal, all the other passengers were on the plane waiting for the twelve late passengers to board the plane for the 11 hour and 45 minute flight to Frankfurt arriving there about 10:00 A.M. German time.

After arriving in Germany, there was a few hours of layover before the plane to Copenhagen was scheduled to depart. On the flight to Copenhagen the flight attendants served a meal that consisted of a variety of cold cut meats. When Roy took a bite of a piece of meat that not only looked different but tasted different than any other meat that he had seen or eaten, he thought to himself that the meat might be horse meat, so he didn't eat any more of it. As the plane was descending into Copenhagen, one could see a beautiful sight of sailing boats with their white sails on the Baltic Sea.

After going through immigration and customs, Glenn, his mother, and father were there to greet Rena and Roy.

When Rena and Roy went to get their luggage, it had not arrived. When they inquired about it, they were told that the luggage was still in Germany. The airline company gave each of them a kit that contained a toothbrush, toothpaste, comb, soap, and deodorant. The next day their luggage arrived at their hotel. Glenn's parents took them to their hotel and picked them up every day to show them Copenhagen and other places in Denmark. One day, Glenn and his parents took Rena and Roy to Tivoli, an amusement park in Copenhagen with several different rides. Glenn said that Tivoli is translated into English as ditch. Tivoli was a very fun and educational place to visit. The family took Rena and Roy to their summer home on the beach for a time of relaxation and conversation. One evening, Glenn's parents took Rena and Roy to their home for a very tasty, home cooked, Danish meal.

When time came for them to leave, Glenn's father took Rena and Roy to the pier of a jet boat to cross the sound to Malmo, Sweden, where Phillip, his brother, Albert, and father, Edward, were waiting for them. As Rena and Roy were going through immigration, all they had to do was hold up their passport to let the officials see it and proceed through the terminal. On the way to where the family was vacationing on an island, Edward stopped at a place where huge stones were placed in the shape of a ship. The father said that some people thought that Vikings had placed the stones there for some reason, but no one really knew how they got there. Phillip's family was staying in an apartment of a church. When they arrived at the apartment, the mother had a great delicious meal for them. While Phillip's mother and Rena went shopping in the town on the island, Phillip and Albert took Roy to the top of a hill to show him the beautiful view of the town below with red tiled roofs and the Black Sea in the background.

When it was time to go to their home, there was not enough room in the automobile for all the passengers and luggage. To solve the problem, Edward took Phillip, Albert, and Roy to the local train station to take the train to Goteborg, which is close to the family's' home in Lerum, where Edward later met them.

One day, Rena and Phillip wanted to go to Oslo, Norway, to see an exchange student that stayed with a family in Rena's neighborhood at the same time Phillip was with Rena and Roy, so Edward took Phillip, Rena, Albert, and Roy to Oslo. One of the first things that they saw when they crossed the border into Norway was an Elvis Presley Museum. Not only did they get to see the Norwegian friend, but they were able to see some other historical sights. There were many other historic places that Edward took Rena and Roy to see. Phillip asked Roy how they were going to Germany. When Roy told him that they had train tickets, Phillip said that a ticket meant that they could board the train, but they may not have a seat. Phillip said that Roy should go to the train station and make reservations to be sure they had a seat from Sweden to London, England. Phillip took Roy to the train station to make reservations that cost an extra sum of money. When Phillip and Roy entered the station, there was a long line at the ticket window. The passengers had to take a ticket number and wait to be called. Phillip found a ticket on the floor that had a higher number than the one to be taken from the machine, but lower than the one already called, so they did not have to wait as long as they would have had to wait, if Phillip had not found the ticket.

Rena and Roy had already made arrangements for Christian, an exchange student from Sweden, to spend the school year 1988 -1989with them. Christian's parents came to Phillip's home to take Rena and Roy to their home in the southern part of Sweden. One day, for lunch, Christian's mother had cold cut meat. Some of it looked like some of the meat on the plane from Frankfort to Copenhagen. Roy asked Christian's father what the meat was. He said that it was horse meat. Then Christian's father said, "I guess that you don't eat horse meat in America."

Roy replied, "No, we don't eat horses in America. We race them." For lunch, Rena and Roy were taken to a famous restaurant on an island off the coast of the Baltic Sea. The restaurant was very crowded with people waiting to order the restaurant's famous Belgium waffles.

The day came for Rena and Roy to say goodbye to Christian and his family. Christian's father drove them to the train station for the trip to Germany. For the first part of the trip, they took the train to a city on the coast to take a ferry to Denmark where a train took them to Copenhagen. There was an eight year old boy with his mother and grandmother on the train. The boy could speak French and English as well as his native language. Roy thought that this was a feat that seldom happened for a young child.

While waiting on the platform by the track for their train to arrive in Copenhagen, a train came into the station on two tracks from where Rena and Roy were. A man and a woman were on the entrance platform of the train. They were so inebriated that they would not get off the train. One of the crew members called the police, and the policemen brought a cart that looked like a grocery cart. After some resistance and loud language by the couple that Rena and Roy were glad they did not understand. The police put them in the cart and carted them away.

It was not long until the train to Hamburg arrived. When the train reached the seaport, it was separated into two sections and backed onto a ferry boat to cross the short distance across the Fehmarn Strait to Germany. (Roy looked at a map and guessed where the crossing was.) After arriving in Hamburg, Rena and Roy took a taxi from the train station to the Dietrich's home where a maid was waiting for them because the Dietrich family was in America looking for a house, while he taught in a medical school. The maid gave Rena and Roy a tour of the house, and told them where and how to catch a city bus. Dr. Dietrich had a model train layout much like Roy had. When Dr. Dietrich visited John at the Vandergrit's house, he had taken one of Roy's model engines home with him to be repaired. But he had not had it repaired. Dr. Dietrich called and told Roy to take the model engine to a nearby hobby shop to have it repaired. When Roy took it to the shop, the salesman asked several questions about the engine as to where Roy got it and how long he had it. He told Roy that the technician who could repair it was on holiday. He told Roy how to get to another shop that might be able to repair it. Rena and Roy took a subway to one place, then had to ride a bus for some distance, and finally had to walk about two blocks to the shop. Someone in the shop was able to repair the engine.

As Roy was paying for it, the cashier asked several questions about how the engine got broken. When Roy told him that his son and friends were playing with it and probably dropped it, the cashier said emphatically, "You don't play with this engine. You put it on a wall."

That statement got the attention of Roy. He thought that it might be worth more money than he thought it was worth. He asked the man, "How much do you think it is worth?"

The man replied, "I don't know, but the man beside you might know because he is a collector of model train engines." When Roy asked that man, he said that it was a collector's engine and worth about $250 to $300. The engine was in a box of HO trains that Roy had bought for $20 from Rick, a student, who asked Roy to buy them. The man asked Roy if he knew anything about an engine that he was trying to find, but Roy did not know anything about it. While in Germany, Rena bought a set of Rosenthal China and had it shipped home.

Rena and Roy left Hamburg by train to travel to Paris through Brussels, Belgium. After arriving in Paris, they went to their hotel by taxi. The taxi driver did not seem friendly at all. She pretended not to understand English, but Roy thought she did.

While in Paris, Rena and Roy visited the Eiffel Tower, Notre Dame Cathedral, the Louvre Museum, and many other sights that brought back memories of Roy when he was stationed in France. They took a tour of chateaus along the Loire River that Roy had already seen but enjoyed them with Rena. Roy wanted to take Rena to see the Versailles Palace, but did not want to go on a tour bus. He asked the tour guide if a train ran to Versailles. She not only said that there was one but told him what subway to take and how to get to it. The palace was a beautiful building along with the outside gardens.

Rena and Roy took a train from Paris to the French coast on the English Channel. They crossed the English Channel on a Hover Craft. When the craft came in, it came all the way on shore. The Hover Craft had the most uncomfortable ride one can imagine. It seemed as if that boat was up and down from both ends and both sides. Roy was very happy when the craft reached England where a train was waiting for the rest of the way to London.

When Rena and Roy were checking into the hotel where their reservations were, they were told that the hotel was having water problems, and they would be sent to another hotel. While waiting for transportation, a young lady, who was very upset, came to the desk complaining about how long it had been since she had a shower and her boyfriend was meeting her that day. While going to the next hotel, the cab driver said something to the effect that the hotel had many problems.

The next hotel seemed to be without problems until bed time. The room had two twin beds. The mattress of the one that Roy chose had a hole in it and was very uncomfortable. The management was told about it but nothing was ever done to correct the situation. Needless to say, that situation was not a pleasant experience. One day, Rena and Roy went on a tour to see the famous

Stonehenge. It seemed almost impossible to understand how those huge stones could be put in place without modern machinery. On the same tour they went to Bath to see the famous hot springs. This was an enclosed area, but no one was allowed to enter the hot water. While Rena and Roy were on a walking tour of London, they saw the changing of the guards at Buckingham Palace. A shopping trip to Harrods was a must.

On the morning of the return trip home, Rena and Roy went to the Victoria Rail Station for the trip to Gatwick Airport for the flight to Atlanta. When they arrived home, they found a newly remodeled kitchen that had been arranged before they left for Europe.

CHAPTER 26

In the spring of 1990, when Roy walked from the school parking lot to his class room, he noticed that his throat was beginning to feel like he had sucked cold wind into his lungs. Also, he noticed that he was getting tired after a brief period of exertion, but he procrastinated going to the doctor. In March, he took a foreign exchange student, Albert, with a school group to Washington, D.C. and walked to several places in the nation's capital.

About a week later, he walked with Albert up a steep hill to the top of Iroquois Park. While he was mowing his lawn, he began to have the same feelings in his throat and was getting tired more quickly.

When he told Rena that he ought to see the doctor, she said, "You saw a throat specialist before, and he said that there wasn't anything wrong."

Roy replied, "This is different than before." He called the doctor and made an appointment for the following Monday. When he went to the doctor on Monday, the doctor said that his blood pressure was a little on the high side, but because of his family history, he wanted him to have a stress test. The doctor had his nurse to call a cardiologist to make arrangements for an appointment the next day.

Before he went to the doctor on Tuesday in the Southwest Hospital, which is no longer a hospital, he prepared some bills for the Kentucky Railroad Museum. He was the treasurer and intended to put them in the mail after he was through with the stress test. While he was on the treadmill he could see the results on the cardiogram machine printout and thought to himself, that doesn't look very good. About that time, the doctor told his aide to stop the machine and told Roy to stand there until he could get him a room because he was going to have to have surgery. Roy said, "Can I come back this afternoon because I have some business to do?"

The doctor replied, "No, you need a cardiac catheterization and surgery." Roy had to sit in a chair until the admitting office could admit him to the hospital.

Roy called Stuart Middle School and asked the principal if he would tell Rena where he was and that he was being admitted to the hospital. Someone brought her to the hospital, and she was surprised at the situation. However, she was able to mail the bills and take the car home to use for her transportation. They had been riding together to teach in Stuart Middle School.

The next day, a cardiologist performed a cardiac catheterization that showed he had four blockages in his heart and would have to be transferred to Jewish Hospital for heart surgery. On May 3, 1990, he was transferred to Jewish Hospital for a quadruple bypass surgery.

Late that evening, the surgeon went into Roy's room to talk to him about the procedure the next morning. He asked Roy if he had any questions. Roy said that he did not want to be put on life support except for the surgery because he knew where he was going if he did not come through the surgery. The next morning, about six o'clock, a nurse came into the room and gave him a shot.

The next thing he remembers was the staff talking about Unbridled Spirit winning the Kentucky Derby that afternoon. This meant that he had been out for over thirty-six hours and was in the Cardiac Intensive Care Unit. He was hooked to a ventilator that was very irritating to his throat at times and had to be adjusted by a respiratory therapist. When some family members came to see him, someone told them that he didn't feel like seeing them, but he doesn't remember saying that. He was only in the hospital for a week when he was dismissed. He had missed the celebration of Claude and Robin's fiftieth wedding anniversary, but the doctors told him that no damage had been done to his heart.

Two weeks after Roy's surgery, his brother-in-law, Alice's husband, went home to be with the Lord. His funeral was in Mt. Vernon, Kentucky, but Roy could not go because he had not healed enough. He had thought about putting a pillow in front of his chest and going anyway, but he thought better of that action. He has had two cardiac catheterizations since the surgery and four or five stress tests. The cardiologist said that Roy only had high blood pressure and medicine could take care of that.

CHAPTER 27

As Roy stated earlier, after he accepted Christ, he began to have a passion for witnessing for Christ and leading others to Him. There have been many opportunities for Roy to do that, but there are some that were in the prison that he would like to tell about to show how God works and to give Him the glory.

In December of 1990, Roy went to the nearby prison with a group to have a Christmas program for the inmates. The program included choral groups going to the different dormitories to sing for the inmates and then to the chapel for services and refreshments. After this experience, Roy volunteered as a volunteer chaplain until 2014, and the following experiences are from the nearby prison.

One experience is about Cunard Shelton who was an inmate in the prison, and he gave Roy permission to write about this. Roy must start from the beginning to show how God works. This started on Easter Sunday in 1994. A lady who was a nurse at the Taylor Cancer Center in Louisville was in a Sunday school class and requested prayer for a twenty-three-old young man in the reformatory who had visited the cancer center and had terminal testicular cancer. She wanted to know if anyone knew someone who might go see him. There was a lady, Sarah, whose husband, Jim, went into the prison every Thursday with a group of men as volunteer chaplains for services. The nurse gave Cunard's name to Jim's wife.

That following Thursday evening, Jim and Roy received permission to visit Cunard because he was in the medical part of the facility and would not be coming to the chapel program. Jim asked Cunard, "Are you saved?"

He replied, "Yes." Also, he had a Bible that another volunteer had given him. They chatted with him for a few minutes and then, proceeded to the chapel.

Roy volunteered in the chapel during the day on Wednesday and would stop by to see Cunard on the way to the chapel. He always told Roy that he was saved. Then on one visit he told Roy that he had never accepted Christ and was not saved. When Roy asked him why he had told them that he was saved, his reply was, "Someone was coming through the unit giving away Bibles and I wanted one. So I told him that I was saved so that he would give me one."

Roy asked him if he thought about asking Christ into his life. He replied, "I'm just not ready, yet."

As time went on, Roy would stop to see how he was getting along. When Roy asked him if he thought any more about getting saved, his answer was always the same, "I'm just not ready, yet, but I don't want to die in prison." Roy thought, but didn't say to him if you accept Christ you'll get out of prison.

The day after Christmas, when Roy went into the prison, the fog was so thick that the men were on lock down which meant they could not go out on the yard. Roy thought that he would stop and see Cunard. During the course of conversation Roy told him that his brother, Claude, had terminal cancer and that the family did not know how much to tell him. Cunard came back with, "They ought to tell him everything. The doctors told me last May that I only had about a year to live."

Roy said to him, "You have known all this time that you have only a short time to live, and you are not ready to accept the Lord."

Cunard replied, "I'm just not ready, yet." The conversation continued and he told Roy that he wanted to see a psychiatrist, but "they" would not let me see one. When Roy asked him why he wanted to see a psychiatrist, he said that he was being bothered by the situation and he wanted some peace.

Roy looked at him and said, "Cunard, I do believe in psychiatric help, but the peace that you are seeking will not come from a psychiatrist. The peace that you are wanting will only come when you accept Christ as your savior."

He replied again, "Roy, I'm just not ready." By this time the yard had opened up, and after Roy prayed for him, he continued to the chapel.

One afternoon, two weeks later, the chaplain from the prison called Roy and told him that Cunard was in the hospital and was very serious because the family had been called in for a bedside visit. He went on to say that when this happened that the person was not expected to live much longer. He said, "Roy, I know that you have been working with him and might want to visit him." Roy replied that he would go see him the next day.   On Saturday, Roy drove the forty-five miles to Tri County Hospital (name has been changed0 to see Cunard. When Roy asked at the Information Desk for the room number where Cunard was, Roy was informed that the hospital did not have him in the hospital, As far as the information desk is concerned the personnel are not provided the names of inmates. Roy called the Control center in the prison and identified himself and said that he would like to have the room number for Cunard. After Roy was given the room number, he proceeded to the room where he found a security officer outside the door. The officer called and told Cunard that he had a visitor. When Cunard asked who it was, the officer told him that it was a chaplain. Cunard replied, "I can't see him just yet but wait." In a few minutes he said that Roy could enter the room. When Roy went into the room, Cunard had only a towel covering him, and he said that the nurse had given him water to wash with but hadn't come back to give him clean water to rinse himself. Roy told him that he would get him clean water, so he could finish the bath which Roy did and went back outside until he finished his bath.

When Cunard said it was okay for Roy to come in, Cunard had a sheet over him but and one of his legs was shackled above one of his ankles to the bed. After the greetings, the conversation progressed, Cunard said that he had cried that night until his pillow was wet. When Roy asked him why he cried so much, he responded, "I was in so much pain, but the officer would not let the nurse give me any pain medication. He said that all I wanted it for was the dope." Roy thought to himself, if you are not ready to accept Christ now, there is no hope for you.

Roy said, "Cunard, have you thought anymore about accepting Christ into your life?' He answered, "Yes, I have."

Roy asked, "When?"

He asked "Can you come back tomorrow? I have to work something out."

Roy told him that he would be back the next day.

The next day, Roy went back to the hospital, but Cunard had been moved to a security ward that had two locked doors with two security officers inside the ward. There were two or three other inmates in the ward besides Cunard who was still shackled to the bed. After the usual greetings Roy said to Cunard, "Are you ready to ask Christ to come into your heart."

He replied, "Yes."

Roy started to read some scripture to him, but Cunard interrupted Roy and said. "Roy, I know the scripture. I just want to get saved."

At that point Roy led him in a prayer for salvation. When they finished praying and Cunard looked up, Roy could tell by the expression on his face that something had happened in his life.

He said, "I feel a big burden has been lifted off me, and I want to go home. I don't mean the home down here but the one up there."

Cunard improved enough that he was transferred back to the prison hospital facilities where Roy would stop to see him. He began to open up and tell Roy about his life before he came to prison. He told Roy that he was incarcerated for stealing a car and that he had a son in Dayton, Ohio, and gave Roy the phone number for his grandmother. God did grant him his wish. He was given a medical parole in late April. About two weeks went by and Roy called Cunard's grandmother to see how he was getting along. She gave Roy the sad news that he was home for three days and passed away. Roy knew that he was ready to go to his heavenly home where he told Roy that he was ready to go.

A second experience that occurred at the prison was with Alvin who was a young inmate from the northern part of the state. Alvin had come to the chapel on a regular basis, and Roy had talked with him on several occasions about Newport because Roy had lived there. Alvin had gotten a write up for something and was put in segregation. When Roy went to see him, he told Roy that he had become frightened the night before when he read in Revelation about Christ coming, and it really scared him. Roy told Alvin that if he were really saved that he wouldn't have to be afraid. He admitted that he had not accepted Christ. At that point Roy was able to lead him to the Lord.

On another occasion, Roy received a phone call from a lady who wanted him to tell her brother that she was going to come see him soon. When Roy called the control center to see where her brother was, he was told that the brother was in the new nursing facility. When Roy went to the nursing facility, he found an elderly man who was sitting in a chair beside his bed. He was in such bad condition that he could hardly get to his bed from the chair. After Roy gave him the message from his sister and further conversation, Roy asked him if he had ever accepted Christ as his savior, and he replied that he had not. Then, Roy asked him if he would like to know Christ as his Savior. After he said that he would, Roy was able to lead him to accept Christ. Unfortunately, Roy doesn't know what happened to him, but he probably died in the prison. When an inmate dies in the prison and the family does not claim the body, the inmate is buried in the cemetery on the prison grounds.

Ralph is another person from the prison whom Roy was able to lead to the Lord. One Thursday night, Ralph came to the chapel and asked Roy if he would help him call his mother who was in a hospital with heart trouble. The only trouble was that he didn't know which hospital she was in, but thought he knew. When Roy called that hospital, she was not in that one or the next one that Roy called. Roy said to him, "Do you know anyone that might know in which hospital your mother is?" He said that he did, and Roy called that number. Sure enough that person knew. Roy called the hospital and Ralph talked with his mother for a few minutes. She told him that she was getting along better and would soon be dismissed from the hospital.

After the phone call, Roy asked him, "Are you saved?" He replied that he was. Then, Roy asked him how he knew he was saved, he began to tell Roy the things that he had done and that he was a good person. Later on he told another inmate that Roy laughed at him when he said that, but Roy doesn't think that he did. What Roy said to him was that the Bible says that a man must be born again to receive eternal life. With that said, he let Roy lead him in a prayer to accept Christ. The following Monday morning he brought in some of his art work for Roy to see. Roy discovered that Ralph was a good artist and was very faithful to come to chapel on Thursday nights.

A short time later, he finished his time and was released from prison. Even though he had put on his application that he had served time in prison, he obtained a job with a national retail store working in the electronics department and became involved in a local church. Soon after that, Rena said that she wished she knew someone who could paint a mural on the walls of the train room. Roy told her that he knew someone who could do it and got in touch with Ralph. He told Roy that he would be happy to do that for him. Roy had a picture of his home community that consisted of a store, his brother's house, the church which Roy attended, the school house, and the house in which Roy lived. Ralph painted this on the walls of the train room, Roy would feed Ralph and his girlfriend when she came with him because he would not take any pay for painting the wall. About three years later, Roy received a wedding invitation to Ralph's wedding. Of course, Roy went. During the reception. Ralph came to Roy and said," Roy, if it hadn't been for you, I still would be in prison." That certainly was a blessing to Roy. He realized how important the verse of scripture is when Christ said, "For I was a hungered, and ye gave me meat: I was thirsty and ye gave me drink: I was a stranger and ye took me in: Naked, and ye clothed me: I was sick, and ye visited me: I was in prison, and ye came unto me." Matthew 25: 35 KJV.

The Thursday before Christmas 2012, the authorities of the prison let an organization bring extra volunteers to sing carols in the dormitories. As the carolers were going to the dorms, Roy and two more men went to the chapel to prepare the food that the group brought and make coffee. An inmate made an early entrance and started a conversation with Roy. After a conversation about his salvation, Roy was able to lead him to Christ. The inmate said that he was supposed to have gone go to another meeting, but he had a feeling that he should come to the chapel for the night and now he knew why because he accepted Christ into his life.

CHAPTER 28

In March 1995, Roy's brother, Claude, had been ill for a few years from Black Lung Disease that he contracted while working in the coal mines for most of his entire working career. He had become ill with prostate cancer and was in the hospital in Corbin, Kentucky where Roy and Eugene went to visit him. He seemed to be in good spirits and was able to carry on a good conversation and he assured Roy that he was prepared to meet Christ. One of Claude's daughters and husband had stopped by the hospital to see him on their way to a vacation. However, before they arrived at their destination they were notified of Claude's death on March 25, 1995. At the age of eighty, God called him home to be with Jesus.

Eugene had a five bypass heart surgery about 1996 and seemed to be getting along well after the surgery. In February 1998, his automobile became stuck in snow that was in the driveway. After he had been shoveling snow to get the vehicle free, his wife urged him to come in the house to rest a while. When he went into the house he sat down in a chair in the dining room, and she went into another room. Soon thereafter, she heard him fall from the chair. When she went to see about him, he had gone home to be with the Lord on February 4, 1998. He had accepted Christ several years earlier and was active in the church where he and his family attended in Lexington. That snowstorm was so bad the funeral director could not find the grave site until a few days after his funeral.

In August 2010, Elijah was so ill that he did not attend the family reunion on Saturday, August 7, Roy called him and he said that he had gone to the Tennessee University Medical clinic and had another appointment with the doctor concerning his heart. The night before the appointment on August 25, 2010, the Lord called him home. He had made a profession of faith in 1949 and was baptized into the Buffalo Baptist Church. In the late fifties, while he was stationed at O'Hare Air Force Base outside Chicago, he met his wife to be who was a Jehovah Witness. Roy doesn't know how involved he actually was in the church. During the memorial service the minister stated that he knew Elijah had put his trust in Jesus. His family had him cremated and put his ashes inside a large grandfather clock.

On Sunday afternoon of April 7, 2013, Roy had a nagging feeling that he ought to go see Jennifer who lived outside Milford, Ohio, but because it was getting late, he decided to go another time. The next day one of his nephews called him to tell him that his mother had to be hospitalized the night before because of kidney failure. When Roy called his brother-in -law to see when a good time would be to come visit her, he said that she didn't want any visitors and had run the family out of her room the night before. She felt so badly that she didn't feel like seeing anyone. After discussing when would be the best time to come to see her, the time was set for Thursday, April 11. Early Wednesday morning, Roy's phone rang and he had a feeling that his sister had gone to be with Jesus. Sure enough, it was his nephew who told him that Jennifer had passed away that night. Jennifer was interred in the Milford Cemetery.

Roy thought that his cousin, whom he had not seen in about fifty-five years, but they had talked on the phone, might be at the wake. Roy asked one of his nephews if he knew his cousin. He replied that he did and pointed him out. They were happy to see one another again. Roy's cousin and Eugene were more of the same age. The cousin's brother, was killed in a plane crash in California during WWII while he was in the Army Air Corps.

CHAPTER 29

Roy's daughter, Letha, went to a university in the Northeast where she met a young man and after dating for several months became engaged. Then, on June 13, 1992, the wedding was in the Northeast. Her wedding gown had a very long train that her twin nephews carried down the aisle. After the initial part of the ceremony, as Roy turned around to step over the train to go to his seat, he stepped on it as she took her first step to go up the steps to the platform. The audience heard a ripping sound as the train fastened to the gown with Velcro came loose and fell on the carpet. The groom's father who was sitting next to the aisle reached down, picked up the train, folded it, and put it beside him just as if it were planned. Roy felt awful for the incident, but his daughter was happy that it happened because the movements on the platform was easier to maneuver than having to deal with the long train.

At first, the couple lived in the Northeast but later moved to another state. Where she had a job with a mental health facility. In August 1993, she had her first child which was Roy's first granddaughter and fifth grandchild. Finally, the couple decided to move back to the Northeast where she had her son.

Letha became ill and was in a hospital for several days. Her mom and dad stayed in a motel while they were in the city to visit their daughter.

Between visiting hours, her husband did allow them to visit the children in their home. The removal of all the wedding pictures from the hall walls were very noticeable to them and they suspected that he was planning on divorcing their daughter, but they never said anything to her. When she was hospitalized, her husband's parents helped him care for the two children.

In early March 1998, Letha's husband called her parents and asked if one of them could come and watch their daughter for a few days because she was ill. A decision was made that Roy would be the one to go. While Roy was there, Letha had to go back into the hospital. Because Roy's return plane ticket was not for two or three days later, he stayed until the day of his flight and was able to visit her in the hospital.

On March 17, 1998, while the daughter was still in the hospital, her husband came for a short visit. About a half hour later, sheriff's deputies delivered divorce papers to her. She said that she could not remember him mentioning a divorce to her. She called her parents about eleven o'clock that night in tears and with great disbelief. The documents stated that she could only see her children for four hours after the first divorce hearing and then never see her children again.

Because she nor her parents did not know any attorneys in the area where she was, Roy called a national organization in which he was member to get the name of an attorney for her. When he called the number, he was told that the attorney was not available and would not be in for another day or two, but that another attorney was in the office. As time was of the essence, the date of the first hearing was set for March 27. Roy decided to go with the available attorney. The attorney went to the hospital to talk to her and get some facts. When Rena and Roy saw the attorney in his office, he asked, "Does she always seem as sedated and non-responsive as she does now?"

Roy responded, "She is like that now because the doctor has her on so many Medications" Letha's attorney advised her not to go to court but let her parents and a governor appointed children's advocate represent her.

Letha had volunteered in an office where the advocate worked and she told his daughter that her parents could stay at her home when they would come to the city. What a great blessing that was because it saved them many motel bills. A lasting friendship developed from the experience with the advocate and her family.

After both sides presented their case in the first hearing, the judge's decision was that she could see her children in their home for the four hours that day with her parents and appointed the advocate as a supervisor of the visits. He said that she could have her children every other weekend or twice a month until the final hearing to be held in November with a stipulation that the children could not be taken out of the state. Rena told his daughter, "I'll see that you will be able to see your children twice a month." His daughter looked for her journals where she had written her innermost thoughts, but she could not find them because they had been given to her husband's attorney and was used against her in the court hearing. Twice a month, Rena, his daughter, and Roy would make about a fourteen hour drive or fly to see the children. They would pick up the children on Friday afternoon and take them to the advocate's home where they would spend their time with the children until it was time to return them on Sunday.

Rena who went to be with the Lord on June 11, 2011 had a very difficult time accepting the divorce. All she wanted to talk about was how the son-in-law had mistreated her daughter. Every time that Rena and Roy went anywhere as soon as she was seated in the car she began to talk about the situation. Also, she talked about it to any one that would listen. One day, as they were going somewhere, she kept talking and talking about what the judge should be told. Finally, Roy said, "Rena, I can't take any more. Can you talk about something else?"

She replied, "You mean I can't say what I think?" Roy knew that she would want to talk about the divorce all the way home after the final hearing in November. He bought her an airline ticket for the return trip on the pretense that she needed to have enough time to prepare some food items for the special dinner which would be two days after the final divorce hearing.

The final divorce hearing was on November 24, 1998, which was on a Tuesday. To understand the situation that was stacked against Letha, one must look at the circumstances. Letha's attorney told her that her husband's attorney and the judge were smoking buddies in a nonsmoking courthouse, and his attorney's legal secretary was a close friend of her husband's family. Of course, Letha was an out of state woman. What chance for a fair outcome did she have in a situation like that?

During the hearing, the husband's side went first as witnesses as Rena and Roy sat outside the courtroom. Because Timmy was not going to be called as a witness, he was allowed to be in the courtroom during the entire trial.

Roy was the first witness for Letha. The attorney asked him what he would do if he were in the husband's place. Roy replied that he thought that he had enough friends that would help him, and said emphatically that he would not get a divorce.

Rena was the next one to be a witness. It seemed like the attorney treated her like she was a criminal being prosecuted, but she could defend herself. The children's advocate was a witness for Letha also. The hearing lasted until late in the afternoon, and the judge delayed making any decision until the next day.

Of course, Rena wanted to stay until the next day to return home. The airlines were called to cancel her flight. Therefore, the money was allowed to be used on another flight.

On Wednesday, as one could expect, the daughter's case was the last one to be heard. The judge made the following decisions: granted the divorce, gave the custody of the children to her husband, and left the visitation rights as they were to have the children's advocate to supervise the visitation.

It seemed to Roy that her husband's attorney led the judge to believe that his daughter's parents were not capable of supervising the children or would take them out of state, and it would be a problem to have them returned home. This ruling was a great relief to Letha because she would be able to see her children and have a close relationship with them.

According to court records, the judge ordered that her journals be returned to her. Not only did her husband return the original journals, but he gave her a copy that was bound together as in a book. Many places were underlined which the attorney had used against her in court but had not used anything that would be detrimental to her husband. To Roy's recollection, her attorney did not have a copy that should have been provided to him. The judge gave her certain items that had to be stored until a truck could be used to take them to her home.

By the time that she saw her children that afternoon and took items to a storage place, the time was late in the afternoon. Letha's family had to drive all night to return home in time to have Thanksgiving Dinner at home.

While driving back, Rena did a great deal of talking about the case but nodded off to sleep every once in a while. The special dinner was held late in the afternoon. During the dinner, Rena began to talk about the trial. One of the others said "If that is all you are going to talk about, why don't you go somewhere else to eat." She left the table and went to another part of the house to finish her meal.

CHAPTER 30

There came a time when the children's advocate could not be the supervisor because she was working on a degree in social work and had to be gone on weekends for conferences. Letha had to go back to court to get someone else to be the supervisor. This time a different judge who had been a middle school teacher and knew what it was to teach and supervise that age children. She let one or both of Letha's parents, or the advocate be the supervisor. As time passed the advocate moved to another city and Letha had to go back to court to get another supervisor. This time, the judge ruled that her ex-husband's parents or one or both of her parents could take turns being the supervisor. For some time, Letha would stay with his parents while visiting the children but that was a mental strain on Letha. Her parents decided that they would do the supervision all the time. Sometimes only one of them would accompany Letha, and sometimes both of them would accompany her. They would pick up the children at 5:00 P.M. on Friday afternoon and stay in a motel and return them on 5:00 P.M. on Sunday. If only one of the parent's accompanied Letha, they would make the trip by flying.

Sometimes this was an ordeal like missing connecting flights or cancelled flights.

Roy and Letha had to spend one night in Cleveland, Ohio because the plane from The Northeast to a connecting airport had to go into a holding pattern because of bad weather that limited take offs and landings in the connecting airport. After their plane landed and as they were going to the gate of the flight to Louisville, Letha saw the gate personnel close the door to the ramp to the plane. The lines for rebooking were long because of the number of missed flight connections. The man who was rebooking their flight said, "The best I can do for you is to get you to Cleveland where you can spend the night and get an early flight to Louisville tomorrow." On the way to Cleveland the weather was so bad that the pilot had to take the plane in a much longer route than usual to get there. They had to spend one night in Baltimore, when the pilot noticed a malfunction of a slat before turning on the runway and had to return to the terminal to change planes that was not available until the next day.

After a plane ticket had been purchased for Rena for one visit to see the children, she fell and broke one of her ankles and could not make the trip. Roy had to book another flight on a different airlines which returned through Chicago. After arriving in Chicago, the passengers were notified that their flight to Louisville had been canceled from the originating airport because the weather was so bad. While Letha returned home on time on one flight, Roy had to spend the night in Chicago and came home the next morning.

Rena and the daughter were on one flight that was within fifteen or twenty minutes from reaching Louisville and had to return to the originating airport because of a malfunction on a part of the plane. On another occasion, they were on a flight that had to go into a holding pattern because there were tornados on both the south end and north end of Louisville. Then the flight was directed to Nashville for refueling. When the plane was ready to leave, the area became under a tornado warning and they had to spend a night in a hotel until the next day. As soon as they arrived at the hotel they had to go into a storm shelter.

Another time, the daughter and Rena were on a flight headed for the Northeast where they had to transfer to another flight, but when the plane reached the end of the runway in Louisville, they had to return to the gate to let some of the passengers with dogs off because there were too many dogs on the plane from a dog show that was held a few days before.

Roy thinks that God used one unusual circumstance to let him lead a lady to accept Christ as her Savior. One Christmas, Letha asked her ex-husband if she could have her children between Christmas and New Year's Day. When he refused, Roy was able to buy three fairly cheap roundtrip airline tickets from an airlines from another airport through Cincinnati and another airport for the weekend of Friday, Saturday and returning on Sunday. About a week later the ex-husband changed his mind, and said that she could have them for the week. Roy then bought tickets just for the daughter and Rena for the week, and Roy used his ticket just for the weekend. On the returning flight to Cincinnati, the airlines sold the aisle seat where Rena usually sat to a lady passenger. This left an empty seat between her and Roy. During the flight one of them started a conversation about where they were going, and one subject led to another. When Roy told her that he was a volunteer chaplain at a prison, she told him that her grandfather was a minister. They had a further conversation about him, and when Roy asked her if she had ever accepted Christ as her Savior, she replied, "No."

There was more conversation and Roy asked her, "Would you like to accept Christ."

She replied, "I thought that you would never ask." Therefore, Roy had the opportunity of leading her to a saving knowledge of Jesus Christ. This event would not have happened if Letha's ex-husband had not changed his mind. Roy believes that the providence of God was in this event.

When Letha had her children for the week, they would rent a cabin in a resort camp where there was good fishing or go to a farm that had some good fishing ponds. Sometimes all of Roy's family including grandchildren would go to be with the children. The cousins got a chance to bond with one another on these occasions.

CHAPTER 31

Beginning about 1965, there was a volunteer organization in Louisville called Operation Appreciation. However, Roy did not learn about Operation Appreciation until 2006. This organization brought soldiers from Fort Knox to a church in the area for about three hours on a Saturday night. Sometimes there would be as many as five hundred soldiers in their last two or three weeks of Army Basic Training. The first hour was very funny entertainment that the soldiers volunteered to do themselves. The second hour was a time of praise and worship. After the praise music, some of the soldiers would give their testimony of what God had done in their lives. Then, one of the volunteers would give his testimony of how God had worked in his life after they had accepted Christ. This person had usually been on drugs or alcohol, or both and had a marriage that was ready to be dissolved through a divorce. The director who had been an atheist would also give his testimony of how he came to know Christ as his Savior. He would give a short sermon on how God would not let sinners into Heaven unless they had been born again. Then, he would use scripture to explain how everyone was a sinner and needed to accept Christ as their Savior. During the last hour the soldiers were given an opportunity to have prayer with a counselor for anything with which they might be having a problem. There would be several soldiers that would go for prayer because they were having problems adjusting to Army life. Some would go because of sick family members. Others would go because they wanted to accept Christ into their lives. Sometimes a counselor may have only one soldier, but other times a counselor may have as many as three or four soldiers. While the soldiers were with the counselors, the others would go to an area where they would have a meal of hot dogs, chips, other kinds of snack food, and a soft drink, or socialize. Over the years, hundreds of soldiers accepted Christ into their lives. In the spring of 2010, the powers that be decided that the soldiers needed more training than letting them come to Operation Appreciation. As a result, the soldiers were not allowed to come anymore. About that time, the Army moved basic training from Ft. Knox to other basic training camps. These are some of the experiences that Roy had while ministering to the soldiers.

On November 10, 2007, at one of the local churches before the program began, one of the privates came to Roy and started a conversation. When Roy asked him about his salvation, he assured Roy that he was saved, and that he had been witnessing to two of his buddies. During the third hour, after he had counseled one soldier, Roy went downstairs to the fellowship area, and one of the first men that Roy saw was the private talking to his battle buddies. Just then, another young soldier came into the group. The private introduced Roy to the soldier and said that he was one of the buddies that he was telling Roy about. After sharing the gospel of Jesus Christ with the private, he accepted the Lord. Just then, another man came into the group. The private said, "This is Ray the other buddy that I was telling you about." Ray told Roy that he had been saved several times. (A red flag went up.) Roy asked him again when he had truly surrendered his life to Christ, and he said that he couldn't remember.

Roy replied, "If you pray, and ask the Lord into your heart and really mean it, you will remember it."

By this time, the men had started to get in formation to leave, so there was not much time left. In the few minutes they had, the young soldier prayed to get right with God once and for all, and he trusted in Christ alone for eternal life. As he turned to leave he said, "Roy, I'll never forget this day." Roy had spent so little time with him that Roy couldn't even remember his face after he left. The seed had already been sowed for these two soldiers.

Two weeks later, Roy, Rena, and his daughter were at the airport to pick up her two children who were coming from their home to help their grandparents celebrate their fiftieth wedding anniversary. Roy noticed several young men in uniform waiting for their flights. As Roy approached the group to ask one of the men if he had come to Operation Appreciation, the soldier said, "You are Roy."

When Roy replied. "Yes."

He replied, "November 10, Roy I'll never forget that day." Then, he told Roy that things had gone much better for him in training and things had not been the same for him since he had been saved. He went on to tell Roy that he was scheduled to go to Maryland by bus, but that there were too many soldiers for the bus, and he was chosen to be one of them to go on a commercial airlines. The providence of God is wonderful. Roy certainly felt blessed after this.

On January 16, 2010, after the praise service, Roy had witnessed to a soldier who accepted the Lord. Roy went into the room where the men had eaten and were fellowshipping. He noticed a soldier just standing alone in the center of the room. Roy approached him and introduced himself and asked him where his home was.

He said, "Kentucky."

Then, Roy replied, "Where in Kentucky?"

By this time Roy knew his first name.

He replied, "Corbin."

To this, Roy responded, "Which part of Corbin, Whitley County, Laurel County, or Knox County?" Jeff was surprised that Roy knew that Corbin was in three counties.

When he asked Roy how he knew that, Roy told him that he grew up in Whitley County in Buffalo between Rockhold and the Cumberland Falls Road.

When he told Roy where he went to church, Roy told him that he had the opportunity of preaching in that church back in 1955. He told Roy that both his father and grandfather were preachers. Roy knew that all preacher's kids are not angels and procrastinate about accepting Christ.

Roy: "Jeff, are you saved?"

Jeff: "No."

Roy: "Jeff, wouldn't you like to accept Christ?"

Jeff: "Yes."

Roy: What about now."

Jeff: "Yes."

When he looked up, after saying the Prayer for salvation, Roy knew that Jeff was a new creature in the Lord. Roy told him that he was going to Williamsburg the next Saturday to attend one of his nieces' fiftieth wedding anniversary. Jeff asked Roy if he would stop by and say hello for him to his mother and father. He told Roy that his father was director of a Christian radio station in that area. Of course, Roy agreed. Sometime during the conversation, he asked Roy if he knew his grandfather Gilbert. At that particular moment Roy could not remember a Gilbert because he was thinking of an older person who might live in Corbin. Roy showed him some pictures that he had taken when he was in Europe while he was in the Army. This drew the attention of three other soldiers who wanted to see the pictures. This gave Roy an opportunity to witness to the three soldiers who accepted the Lord. Roy took a picture of Jeff as well as many men to whom he witnessed and other group pictures and sent a copy of them to the men. The next Saturday, Roy stopped by to see Jeff's parents at the radio station. He introduced himself as Roy Vandergrit. When Roy showed them a picture of Jeff and asked if they knew him, one of them said that he had already sent them a picture and told them that he had accepted the Lord. His father said that he had talked to Jeff several times, but he would not respond to accepting Christ. His mother said that she cried and cried for joy when she read the letter.

Both of them were very thankful that Jeff had accepted the Lord and would not have to worry about something happening to him and his not being saved. Sometime during the visit, Roy mentioned that he had grown up in Buffalo. Jeff's mother asked Roy if he knew Gilbert. At first he told her, "No." A thought went through his mind I think she thinks my last name is Gilberts. Like a bolt of lightning, he did know a Gilbert. When he asked her if Gilbert had a brother Lewis and one named Albert, she replied that he did. He did know Gilbert because Lewis and Albert grew up in Buffalo at the same time as Roy did. Gilbert was much younger and Roy never knew him like he did Lewis and Albert. On Easter Sunday of April 2010, Roy was visiting his home church and a terminal ill nephew who lived close to the church. Roy asked his niece, who lived close by the church, if she knew where Gilbert lived. She told Roy where and how to get to his house.

When Roy introduced himself, Gilbert said, 'So you're the man that Jeff has been talking about." Roy told him that he would like to know where Jeff was now. Gilbert told Roy that Jeff had gotten out of the Army on some technicality, and that he was home in Corbin. After Gilbert told Roy the address, Roy went to Jeff's home. They were both elated to see each other. Jeff introduced Roy to his mother, sister and two brothers. At one point one of Jeff's brother and Roy were left alone when Roy had the opportunity of witnessing to him and he accepted Christ. What a blessing!

There were many other soldiers that God blessed Roy with the opportunity of leading them to accepting

Christ into their lives, but the one that probably affected Roy the most is Boyd White. After the worship service was over and the men were socializing Boyd and Roy were just talking when Roy asked him, "Boyd, if you died tonight, what percent are you sure you would go to heaven?" Roy doesn't remember his exact answer or the rest of the conversation, but Boyd was not saved; however, he did let Roy lead him in a prayer and he accepted Christ in his life.

Boyd told Roy that he would be staying at Ft. Knox to do his Advanced Infantry Training and would be there for Thanksgiving Day. Roy told him that if he could get away for Thanksgiving dinner that he would pick him up and bring him to his house for dinner. Roy knows the feeling of being in the Army and someone inviting him into their home for a Christmas meal, but Boyd was not allowed to leave base that day. After he graduated Advanced Infantry Training, they continued to keep in touch via email even after he was deployed to Iraq. The last email Roy sent was not delivered for whatever the message said. Roy sent another email and the same message came back. Roy thought the worst had happened to Boyd but prayed that it had not. He had told Roy that he was from a western state and that he visited his father in another state. A few days went by and Roy went online and found that Boyd had been killed in Iraq, and that his funeral had been held in that western state. This was very sad for Roy. He was blessed to know that Boyd knew Christ as his savior and that the two will meet someday in glory.

CHAPTER 32

In the spring of 1993, Roy was riding with some of his friends to the nearby prison when one of the men asked if anyone would like to go to Russia on a mission trip. This perked up Roy's attention because several years earlier he had read a book, about a man who had smuggled Bibles into Russia. He had a desire to go to Russia after Communism had fallen, but he would not have to smuggle the Bibles into Russia. After receiving answers to several questions about the cost and timing of the trip, he gave the possibility of going some serious thought. He knew that he would be retiring in June, from the Jefferson County Public Schools, and would receive pay for one hundred twenty-six sick days that he had not taken while teaching.

After consulting with his wife, he decided that he would go. He contacted the pastor who was getting the mission trip together and was given the information that was needed. The pastor had several meetings to prepare for the trip. There were about twelve members of the team who were going to have a life changing experience.

The departure day finally arrived for the most blessed experience that one could imagine. The group met at the

Louisville International Airport to begin the long overnight plane trip to Moscow, Russia. After the group checked in, said goodbye to loved ones, and went through security at the terminal, they proceeded to the Delta gate to board the regional jet to Cincinnati for the first part of the journey. After the Com Air's short flight to the Cincinnati airport in Hebron, Kentucky a bus took them to Delta's main terminal for the connecting flight to Chicago's O'Hare Airport. While going to the departing gate in Chicago the group had to go through Immigration and Customs. When it came time to board the KLM 747 plane to Amsterdam, the passengers were taken by bus to the plane. There was a set of steps to the front part of the plane, and another near the middle of the plane. After all the passengers were on board, the plane left about 5:00 P.M. for the overnight flight to Amsterdam. There was a television monitor on board that kept the passengers informed about the outside temperature, the location of the plane, and a movie. Two meals were served between Chicago and Amsterdam. After the plane landed in Amsterdam, the group went to another gate for the final flight to Moscow. As the plane descended into the Moscow airport, one could see pine forests. Before landing, the flight attendant came through the plane to have the passengers fill out forms for the Russian Customs and Immigrations.

As soon as the group got through customs and immigration, one of the men took out his guitar and the group sang gospel hymns until the tour guide came to greet the group. Of course, this got the attention of some of the passengers in the terminal. The group could not enter the country as missionaries but as tourists. The guide led the group to a bus that would be the mode of travel for three days.

On the way into Moscow from the airport, the guide told about how close the Germans came to the city before they were stopped. There were many other interesting historical sights that were pointed out to the group. One place was a McDonald's Restaurant that she said was the largest one that McDonald had; however, Roy had heard that there was a McDonald's in Oklahoma over Interstate 44 that also claimed to be the largest one. Someone noted that the one in Oklahoma had more space, but the one in Moscow seated more people.

When the day of touring was completed, the group went to a very beautiful hotel for the night. Likewise, a very beautiful view could be seen from the window of Roy's room. Across the broad street, there looked like an entrance to a subway. Beyond that was a very tall structure that looked like some kind of communication tower. Someone said that it was the tallest structure in the world at that time in 1993. Roy made a video of the street and surrounding area.

The next day began with breakfast in the hotel. There was a variety of food, but Roy had hot oatmeal because he had to watch his diet. The tour guide met them for the day's activities. She took the group to many historical places. She took them to hear a musical group in a building that had been a Christian church. The major instrument was a balalaika, a Russian instrument that is shaped like a triangle and usually has three strings, but the band had different versions of it, and everyone enjoyed the performance.

The time finally came to go to the railroad station for the overnight train to Donetsk. When the group arrived at the station, about four men loaded the luggage on a huge board and carried it to the platform where the train was. This saved the team members of having to fight the crowd with the luggage. Two members were assigned to each compartment on the car where they would be sleeping. Most of the members had never ridden on a train, unlike Roy who had ridden many trains in America as well as Europe. Roy's train partner was an elderly man from a town south of Elizabethtown. He told Roy that he was a pilot and had his own plane. He told Roy about a frightening experience when he was caught in a situation above the clouds and was having a difficult time of finding a break in them to land.

The journey to Donetsk was very educational for Roy. Sometimes there were double tracks, and the trains did not have to go on a passing track, but other times, it was a single track, and the train would have to go on a siding for an oncoming train. Instead of having electronic signals or semaphores for signals, there were workers, mostly women, stationed every so often with the different colors on boards that were shaped like a large Ping-Pong paddles. Green means proceed on to the next signal. Yellow means go ahead but be prepared to stop if the next signal is red. Red means stop until the signal turns yellow.

At most of the train stations, many venders were there selling garden or fruit produce: potatoes, onions, breads, apricots, and various other items. Also, between the stations, there would be platforms for people to come to wait on a train that would stop for them. Roy was reminded of the movie, "Fiddler on the Roof", when some of them walked to catch the train because they were forced to leave their homes.

Roy had a very difficult time of going to sleep on the train because the brothers in another compartment played a guitar and sang gospel songs until late in the night. When the group arrived in Donetsk, a tour bus had been arranged to take them to a hotel. After checking into the hotel, a Senior Pastor who was over several churches, met them and divided them into groups of three to send them to other cities to minister to churches in that area.

Three groups were taken to the cities where they were going to minister, but Roy's group had to stay the night in the hotel until the next day to go to their church in another city. As they were settling in their room, they discussed what they should do. They decided that they should get on their knees and pray about the situation. After they prayed, one of the men saw a building with writing in Russian. He looked in his *Russian-English Dictionary* and discovered that it was some kind of youth building. As they started toward the building, they met four young teenagers outside the hotel. The men struck up a conversation with them. One of the youths asked the men if they had cigarettes. Of course, the men did not have any cigarettes, but they had something much more important to offer them. They had gospel tracts specially printed to be used in Russia and Ukraine. The tracts had been printed lengthwise on legal size paper and divided into three parts. On one part was the English of the plan of Salvation and the Prayer for salvation in English. The middle section had illustrations. The third section had the plan of Salvation and the Prayer for salvation printed in Russian.

During the conversation one of the young men who looked to be about 15 or 16 left the group and went somewhere else. The pastor and the other man led the other three to the Lord. Then, all of them walked across the street toward the building. There the young man who left the group rejoined them. After he entered the group, Roy was able to use the tract to lead him to the Lord. When he looked up after accepting Christ, he had tears in his eyes and there was no doubt in Roy's mind that the young man had an experience with Jesus Christ. To know that God can work through language barriers was a great blessing to Roy.

When it was time to retire for the night, a band was playing loud music directly under Roy's room. He could not understand the television, and he needed to go to sleep. He prayed that the band would become quieter. About five minutes later, God answered his prayer when a thunder storm came and the band had to go inside.

The next day, a driver that had been arranged took them to the city where they would be participating in the Saturday and Sunday worship services. On the way, the driver stopped at the home of the Senior Pastor to get Bibles for which the members had paid. The auto was already full with the team's luggage, so the Bibles were put in every nook and cranny that could be found. While getting the Bibles, the pastor's wife told the team that she and her husband had attended a Bible college in Illinois.

When the group arrived at the church, they met the pastor of the church and some other men. The team was taken to a farm house where it seemed that two families resided. Also, some members from the church were there. The entire group was involved in making bricks like the children of Israel made in Egypt. They had forms for the size of bricks. The younger children mixed clay and straw together with their feet. Then, this mixture was packed into the forms and put in the sun to dry. From the looks of the children, they really enjoyed their part of the work because they had mud all over them. Sometimes they would flip the mixture on one of the other young people and laugh. When Roy asked why straw was used, he was told that the straw was partially hollow and made for better insulation than a solid brick. One of the young boys was wearing a Cincinnati Bengals tee shirt that made Roy wonder how he obtained it. When it began to rain, everyone went into the house. The walls and ceiling of the house had been wallpapered. There was an older man who had just come from the doctor. He told the family that the doctor told him that he had an incurable heart condition, and the doctor could not help him.

When lunch time came, the group was seated at a very long table. Before they ate, everyone stood, and one of the Ukraine men asked the blessing. There were many kinds of delicious food. During the meal, many questions were asked both of the Ukrainians and Americans. After the meal, everyone stood while one of the men prayed. One of the men said that when people prayed that they either stood or knelt. After the meal, the team was driven to the church where the team was visiting.

A tall stockade type fence surrounded the church with a small parking lot.

Someone said that during Communism that their pastors were severely persecuted. One of the pastors was killed when the guards let dogs attack him. After the other two men gave their testimony, the pastor that was with the team did the preaching. Everything had to be interpreted. After the services, a baptismal service was held about a mile from the church. It was raining so heavily that the congregation had to wait in the church before walking to a river where the baptismal service was held. There were two small portable changing booths where the candidates and the pastor could change clothes. The pastor of the church let the American pastor with the team baptize the candidates. As each candidate started to go into the water he or she was given a bouquet of flowers. When that person went under the water, the flowers were released. This was a beautiful sight. When Roy asked about the flowers, he was told that during Communism when flowers floated down the river, that people could see them and know that people had accepted Christ and were baptized. Several times during the baptismal service, the pastor would look toward the top of the river bank as if to see if anyone was observing that maybe should not be there. Also, Roy could see trains a short distance away.

After the Baptismal services, the three were taken to their host family for the night.

The mother was a doctor who had a great evening meal. She served each man enough food that was enough for all three of them. The father was an electric power plant manager, and they had a young teenage daughter.

There was a very small refrigerator in the kitchen. Some of the leftover food was put in heavy pots and set outside on a balcony where it was cooler than in the apartment

After the evening meal, the driver took the three team members and another young man to a library for a discussion of some kind. One of the men gave a long history lesson of Ukraine and the men asked a number of questions about America. The young man pointed out some pictures hanging around the walls of the library that someone had painted. The paintings began with the birth of Jesus and others depicted several events in His life and ended with His ascension. One must realize that this was only about three years after Communism fell and this was a public library. Can a scene like this be found in Christian America in a public library? Roy doubts it very much.

When the team went to bed, two of the men slept on a double bed and Roy slept on a cot. Roy thinks that the interpreter slept on a couch.

After everyone was up the next morning, the doctor asked if any one of the three had any medicine for a sore throat. She explained that she had a sore throat but did not have any medicine for it, and that there was very little medicine in Ukraine. None of the team members brought any medicine with them. When one member asked what she did for medicine, she replied that herbs were used for most medicine.

The Sunday morning service was a very memorable one. Again the visiting pastor preached that morning. The young man who filmed the baptismal service wanted to film the church service. During the service, Communion was taken. Instead of grape juice like Roy was used to using, real wine was used. Instead of using small communion cups, one chalice was used and passed from one partaker to another. The last song that was sung was "How Great Thou Art". Roy looked all over the church to see where the cameraman was to video the song because it was so beautiful, but he didn't see him.

After the benediction, Roy looked down and saw the camera at his feet. He had been so engrossed in the service that he had not noticed when the camera was brought to him. The main auditorium and a room in the back were filled to capacity for both of the services. Following the noon meal at the church, the driver took them back to the hotel in Donetsk where the group spent their last night before starting their return trip home.

When breakfast was over the next morning, the tour guide took the group to the train station via more touring of the city for the return trip to Moscow. Everyone related their experiences about where they had gone. One group said that they had gone to a nursing home where there was no medicine. Others told similar stories about their experiences. Roy thinks that his group had the best experience at the church and baptismal services.

Before boarding the train, the group stopped at a sidewalk café to have lunch. The group's train car was the last one of a sixteen car train.

As the train was leaving the area, a large railroad yard of passenger cars could be seen. When the train made a stop at a station, Roy thought that the station and surroundings looked familiar. He was in the vestibule of the train car when a Ukrainian passenger who had too much alcoholic beverages to drink started a conversation with him. The passenger insisted that Roy take him to America. He was so inebriated that he couldn't understand that he had to have a passport and a visa to go to America. Roy decided to go back into the coach and not discuss it any further.

When the train crossed a river a short time later, he recognized the spot where the baptismal service was on the previous Saturday. Because there was not a dining car on the train, the hotel had packed meals to have something to eat on the return trip to Moscow. Roy was disgusted with one of the men when the man threw a bag of trash out the window of the train.

As the train was going up a grade and a curve, one of the ladies said, "Look at that train going up that hill." She was almost in disbelief when Roy responded that it was their train, and they were on the last car. Looking out the window late that afternoon, a beautiful sunset going down over a large field of sunflowers could be seen. This scene reminded Roy of the beautiful gospel song, "A Beautiful Life," written in 1918 by William Golden that Roy learned while singing in church, with the Refrain:

> "Life's evening sun is sinking low,
> A few more days, and I must go
> To meet the deeds that I have done,
> Where there will be no setting sun.
> No setting sun".

That night on the train, it was much quieter than the one going to Ukraine because the brothers did not play their music.

When they arrived in Moscow the next morning, the tour guide took them on a tour to see more of Moscow.

One of the places she took them to see was Lenin's Tomb that is very close to the Kremlin. Roy thought that Lenin looked more like a wax figure than a real human being. He can now say that he saw Lenin, the founder of communism, even though he had been dead for years.

After lunch, the group was taken to the Moscow airport to take an Aeroflot plane to St. Petersburg which was named Leningrad during the communist years and still had that name on one of the buildings. St. Petersburg was a beautiful city. Late one afternoon, their group went to the Temple of the Atheist. While there, a group of young people were visiting. The team began to give out their tracts to the young men and witnessing to them. Roy noticed that one of the men just gave a young man a tract without saying anything to him. Then, Roy had an opportunity to speak with him and asked him if he could explain the tract. After he explained the tract to him, as he read the Prayer for slvation in English the young man read it from the tract. Roy felt that the young man really meant what he had prayed and accepted Christ. This is another example of the gospel crossing language barriers.

The next day, their guide took the group to an historical part of town. At one point, where they passed out tracts as they walked along looking at the sights, one of the ladies decided that she would like to go into a shop just to look around. Roy went in and didn't see anything that he would like to buy. He went back onto the sidewalk to pass out tracts. In a few minutes, a man came from what looked like a courtyard. After greeting him, Roy showed him the tract that he was handing to those who would accept them. He let Roy go over it with him. At the end of the tract, he read the prayer in Russian as Roy read it in English. When he looked up he had a smile on his face. Since Roy had no more Bibles to give him he went into the shop and asked for one from one of the other team members for him to give to the Russian. As he left, he was in the middle of the street he turned around, held up his Bible, and gave Roy a big smile. Roy knew then that he had really accepted Jesus which was a great blessing to him.

The tour guide took the group to a beautiful, famous theater to see the ballet, Swan Lake. Some of the group did not like it, but Roy did. When he was in college he had taken Music Appreciation under Dr. Logeston, who had introduced the class to the ballet, and he thought about her during the performance.

There were many other places that the group saw, but only two will be mentioned one place was Catherine the Great's Palace, which was inside the city and the Winter Palace that was outside the city The Winter Palace has a long history. It was almost destroyed but was rebuilt. All visitors had to wear special coverings over their shoes to protect the floors. A few pictures of the inside of the palaces are on the internet as of February 2015. After returning to St. Petersburg, the group was taken to a very good restaurant for the noon meal. Caviar was served as a side dish to entice the diners to buy small jars of it. Because Roy did not like the taste of fish eggs, he did not purchase any.

After lunch, the group was taken to the airport to get their flight to Amsterdam. After going through customs and immigration, they boarded the plane to Amsterdam with a stop in Helsinki, Finland. Only the passengers whose destination was for Helsinki were allowed to deplane. On the flight to Amsterdam, Roy was looking at the terrain below and saw a huge lake that he thought he recognized from maps and an earlier visit to Sweden. He decided that the plane was over Sweden and mentioned it to the passenger next to him. A few minutes later, the pilot came on the speaker and said that they were over Sweden and told how much longer it would be until landing in Amsterdam where the mission group would be spending the night.

After deplaning, the group was met by a tour guide to escort them during their time in Amsterdam. She took them first to their hotel. There was not much time for touring, but a canal tour of Amsterdam was a must for the group. This brought back memories of when Roy was there in April 1959. That evening meal was at McDonalds. Of course, staying in a very nice hotel was much better than in the hostel where he stayed in April 1959. The following morning when they arrived at the airport, the wind was so strong that one of the runways was closed causing a delay in landings and takeoffs.

On the flight from Amsterdam to Chicago, Roy had a window seat with another man in the seat next to him. It was not long before the two started a conversation. The man told Roy that he and his wife had come to Amsterdam on a flight from England on their way home to Nashville. When Roy told him that he was from Louisville, the man said that his wife's nephew was a school principal in Louisville. Roy asked him where he was a principal. The man said that he didn't know which school. Then Roy asked him the principal's name. When the man told Roy the principal's name, Roy replied, "I can tell you the name of the school because he was my principal." Is this a small world or not?

It was a clear day, and Roy could tell when the 747 was no longer over the Atlantic and the map on the monitor indicated they were over Canada, but it was not long until the monitor was turned off. Roy had studied maps enough and had been to Mackinac Island so he knew when the plane was over it and was heading south just off the eastern coast of Lake Michigan. Roy said to the passenger next to him, "We ought to be coming over Traverse City before long." Just a few more minutes the pilot announced that they were coming upon Traverse City. It wasn't long until the plane banked right to cross Lake Michigan and line up with the O'Hare runway. When the group passed through immigration and customs, they had to go to the terminal where their plane to Cincinnati would be leaving.

After another transfer in Cincinnati to a small propeller plane for Louisville, they were on their last leg home. Waiting for them were families eager to see them and hear their stories of being missionaries for two weeks.

Soon after returning home Roy's first and only granddaughter was born on August 25, 1993.

CHAPTER 33

In 1994, while Roy was working in his shed, he just could not get the experience of going to Ukraine out of his mind. He said, "Lord if you want me to go back to Ukraine, let me find a part time job, so I can save the money to pay the expenses of making the trip." That night about 9:00 P.M. he received a phone call from a friend wanting to know if he would like to teach G.E.D. classes in jail. She said that the Adult Education Department was looking for someone who would not be intimidated by the inmates and she knew that he did prison ministry. That was very exciting to Roy because he knew that was an answer to his prayer. Roy began to teach G.E.D. classes in the Louisville Metro Corrections to save his money to go to Ukraine.

In the spring of 1996, he contacted one of the men from the first trip about returning to Ukraine. Roy discovered a trip was scheduled with an evangelist from Florida to take in August. He was told that the group was taking "over the counter" medication to give to the people that they would be visiting. Roy had a suitcase that he was going to fill with medicine to take with him. After he discussed the trip with his pastor, the pastor told him to bring a box the size of the suitcase, and he would ask the members to fill it with the medicine. The members did a great job of filling the box with all kinds of over the counter medicine.

The time to depart finally arrived. There were several men and women from around the central Kentucky area that Roy met at Louisville International Airport for the flight on Delta Airlines to Atlanta where they would meet others who were going on the trip. One of the members was a seventy year old lady from South Carolina. Another member was a gentleman from Tennessee, who had retired from the Southern Railroad, and was closer in age to Roy than the other members were. The leader of the group was an evangelist from St. Augustine, Florida, who brought along the music director. After boarding the plane, and it taxied to get in line to take off, the pilot came on the intercom to announce that the plane was twenty first in line to take off. It was several minutes before the plane was in the air headed toward Vienna, Austria for the connecting flight to Kiev, Ukraine.

After some time went by, Roy was looking down from the plane. He could see the coastline and a land mass that looked like Long Island. Of course, the monitor confirmed this. Later, he decided to walk on the plane to stretch his legs. He met a young man from the Atlanta area who was taking a group of young people on a mission trip to Romania. He said that his parents were descendants from Romanian immigrants. After further discussing their trips, they prayed for the safety and success of the trips. At one point, the monitor showed the outside temperature was minus forty-one degrees. When arriving in Vienna, the group was directed to the area where the flight to Kiev would be without going through Customs and Immigration.

The flight from Vienna to Kiev was on an Austria Airbus. The breakfast meal on that flight was really delicious. While inflight a flight attendant had the passengers complete forms for the Customs and Immigration that they would have to go through after landing.

A prearranged tour guide meet the group and took them to a nice hotel. After lunch, the guide took them on a tour of Kiev, the capital of Ukraine. The tour took the group to beautiful Saint Sophia's Cathedral and the capital building. Another interesting place was a sidewalk fair that had many different kinds of items for sale. Roy bought some doilies for his wife to use on their furniture.

The man from Tennessee and Roy shared the same room wherever they went. From their room in Kiev, they had a wonderful view of the city. They could see a large sports stadium. Roy could hardly go to sleep that night because not far from the hotel a dog kept barking for a long period of time. He thought that dog would never quit barking. Someone outside the hotel must have been kept awake too because Roy heard a gunshot, and the barking stopped. The next morning at breakfast, some of the others were complaining about the dog.

When time came to go to the train station for the trip to Lugansk, the group was told that there was a miners' strike in the area where the group was going. The miners were blocking the railroad and the trains were not running. They would have to spend another night in Kiev, but they would go the next morning in a van.

The tour guide had nothing planed for that day, so some of them walked to an inside market that had many stalls including an open-air meat market. Roy stopped at a seed and bulb stall where the man could speak some English. He showed Roy a catalog with a picture of Queen of Night Tulips that is such a dark purple that it looks black, and wanted to know if he had any. When Roy told him that he had them, the Ukrainian wanted Roy to send him some bulbs. Roy told him that he had to buy them from the same company in the flower catalogue and couldn't send him any bulbs.

The second night at the hotel was much better than the first one. When the van arrived for the group, Roy wondered how everyone and all the luggage could get into the van. Even though it was crowded, they managed to get in the van for the 11 hour trip. At one point, the driver seemed to have missed a turn and had to change course to get on the right road. It was late in the afternoon when they arrived at the hotel where they would be staying for the next few days.

A lady from southern Indiana across from Louisville had been there for about a month. She had been with an organization to send some heavy medical supplies such as used hospital beds to be used in the hospitals. While the team was in Lugansk, they stayed in a hotel which was about three blocks from where the night services were held. The man from Tennessee had been to Ukraine before, and he went out on his own to visit some of the friends that he had made on his previous trip. He would return for the meals and to sleep. He and Roy got along very well because they could talk trains as well Jesus.

The same senior pastor that was in Donetsk was there to help coordinate the different services. A video was made of him explaining how the churches used the medicine to minister to the people. He said that people would stop by the church to get an aspirin. He explained that a bottle like the team brought might cost a person's salary for a week. While that person was getting the aspirin, someone would witness to that person and possibly lead him or her to the Lord. The team shared the medicine with the pastor but reserved some for a nursing home and a veteran's hospital.

Roy knew from being in Ukraine in 1993 that some hotels did not have hot water during the summer, so he took a small size heater to have some hot water. When the ladies discovered that he had it, they came to borrow it to have hot water to wash their hair. Someone had brought a small water purifier, about the size of a bicycle tire pump to use, so the team would not get dysentery. A person could fill a two liter soda bottle with tap water and then pump that water into another soda bottle. Therefore, no one became sick from drinking the tap water.

Some of the team went to a park where a Vacation Bible School was being conducted by a group of young people on a mission trip from Texas. This group held a service in a theater. There was a difference of opinion with one of the younger members. He told Roy that someone in the group told him that he was too young to be involved with any decision, so he was returning home. Roy felt very badly for him, but he learned later that the young man was pastoring a church in Texas.

There was a missionary family there from the western part of the United States who lived in a house that had at one time been occupied by a man who had an illegal printing press that he used to print Christian material. The missionary gave the following scenario:

> The man had dug a pit in the basement of his home and installed a printing press to print Christian literature. When he was not using the press, the floor looked natural.
>
> The authorities knew that he was printing the material and had searched the house but could not find anything to arrest him. He and his wife had a code that they could use if they were away and police were at their house. One day, the police came when the man was gone and searched the house. As they were about to leave their young child said to them, "You are not very good hunters."
>
> They asked him, "Where would you look?" The child told them where some literature was hidden. The husband called home and his wife gave him the code, so he didn't come home. The mother was arrested.

Roy doesn't know what happened to the man, but after communism fell he was released from prison and the family came to the United States and settled in Washington or Oregon. To have hot water in the summer time, the man who had the printing press had built a platform about 10 feet high and installed a water container. When the water became warm from the sun, a person could take a shower.

The missionary had the local drug store in one of the rooms of the house.

One of his members was expecting a baby. When she went for a checkup, the doctor told her that she needed to have a C-section, but the hospital did not have any medicine to perform the procedure. No one was allowed to visit her in the hospital, but he and some of the members went to see her and stood below her third floor window. She told him what she needed. He went back to the house, got the medicine, and took it back to the hospital. She used a rope to lower a basket for him to put the medicine in. Then she pulled it back to her room for the doctor to use for the surgery.

During part of the day, the team would pass out leaflets about the evangelistic service that night at an auditorium that had been used for communism propaganda lectures. Also, this provided for some personal witnessing.

One day, the team went to a nursing home where one of the members preached a sermon to some of the residents who came to the service. Several of the residents accepted Christ. Some of the medicine was given to the nursing home.

On another day, the missionary's wife took the group to a children's hospital where she had a program for the children in a courtyard. She told Bible stories and played some fun games in which the adults participated. Roy got to talk with one of the mothers. She told him that the situation seemed hopeless because there was nothing that could be done for the children. It seemed that many of the children had some form of cancer. Roy witnessed to her and told her that there was hope in Christ.

Since these children were from many different cities, it could be conjectured that some of the children came from the Chernobyl area. There had been an atomic melt down in Chernobyl where many people died and others were left with injuries. The missionary's wife and two of the ladies were allowed to go into the hospital. They saw two children who were not expected to live very much longer. Before the group left Ukraine, they were told that one of the children had already died.

Later, the team went to a veterans' hospital where some of the medicine was left for the patients. About fifty veterans came to the assembly to hear the gospel preached. Because Roy was a veteran, he had the honor of bringing the message to these veterans. The message had to be translated into the Russian Language. When he gave the invitation and led them in the Prayer for salvation, about thirty-five raised their hand that they had accepted Christ as their Savior. Among those who raised their hand was one of the hospital administrators who came to one of the night services and came forward to make a public decision. Roy was greatly blessed with this experience. Roy was permitted to visit the cardiac ward where there were four patients. The only equipment in the room besides the hand cranked beds were a table and chairs.

The evangelistic services were held in late afternoons not very far from the hotel. Even though all the team members took turns giving their testimony at the services, the evangelist said that he would be the one that would give the invitation. Each night after it was given the team members would give a Bible to everyone that came professing Christ as Savior.

One day, one of the young interpreters who lived across the street from the hotel went with Roy around the neighborhood to make a video. While they were walking, he said to Roy, "Are you going to tell how bad the neighborhood is?"

Roy replied, "No, because that is what some of the magazines did to a region of Kentucky where I live." Then Roy told the young man to take the camera and he could say what he wanted to tell about the area he was filming. This really pleased the young man

During one of the lunch meals, Roy asked the evangelist and music director who were from Jacksonville if they knew Berry Brock who was pastoring a church in Jacksonville, Florida. One of them said that he knew him. He said that he had bad news because Berry had died about two years earlier from some kind of food poisoning. That was sad news for Roy because they had been friends in college and seen each other several times since then.

On July 17, the Senior Pastor told the team at lunch time that a TWA plane had crashed the evening before off the coast of New York and sabotage was suspected.

One member of the team said that he thought one of the men who stayed around the hotel lobby watching the bell boys handle the guests' luggage was part of the Mafia. He said that he saw someone give the bell boy a tip and then this man went to him and the bell boy gave the man some of the tip money. When it was time for check out, Roy gave the tip in the room instead of waiting until they were in the lobby. The lady from Indiana, who was already there stayed sometime longer. Before the team left, she asked if anyone had any bathroom tissue left. She said that she would appreciate it if they would give it to her because she had been there for so long that she was about to run out. Of course, they all obliged.

When the time came to leave Lugansk, the miners' strike had ended, and the trains were running again. The trip to Kiev was by an overnight train which was much better than in the van from Kiev to Lugansk. The train had a dining car on it. Roy noticed that instead of workers signaling the train along the track there were signal lights. What an improvement in three years!

After the train arrived in Kiev the next morning, the group went on to the airport. Security was very tight at the airport. While checking in for the flight to Vienna, the gentleman in front of Roy was told, by the person who was checking him in that his passport had expired, and he would have to go to the consulate to get it renewed. That man was not a very happy traveler. While checking in, Roy was asked many more questions about his luggage than he had ever been asked before.

When the team arrived in Vienna, they were told that they had missed their flight to Atlanta and would have to spend the night in Vienna. The leader said that a hotel room would be either $175.00 0r $250.00, but the airlines would pay for it. After claiming their luggage, they made their way across the street to the $250.00 room hotel. The first thing that Roy saw when he opened the door to his room was a TV that read, Welcome Mr. Vandergrit. The bed had a large down comforter. One of the most welcoming things was a hot shower that was something he had not had in Ukraine. What a blessing it was to have a hot shower.

Sometime in Vienna, the music director said that on the flight from Kiev he sat beside a man who said that he was a nuclear scientist. He was on the team that the government sent to Chernobyl to investigate the "melt down." When he began to report things that should not have happened, he was dismissed from the team. The scientist said that he started reading the Bible to prove that it was not authentic, but the more he read the more he found that it was factual and he became a Christian. What a testimony for Christ!

In the afternoon some of them decided to go into Vienna. While there, they saw St. Stephan's Cathedral which is a very ornate building. In the square, near it, a protest was taking place. On one street was a house with a plaque on it that said Home of Zwingli. Roy recognized him as being a reformer during the Reformation.

The next morning, breakfast was a smorgasbord type of meal. Any kind of breakfast food imaginable was there. After breakfast, it was time to cross the street to the airport to get their flight to Atlanta.

Roy kept his eye on the TV monitor to see where the plane was in relationship to Atlanta. He could tell by looking at the monitor and seeing terrain below when the plane was over Iceland.

While the passengers were deplaning in Atlanta, one of the ladies looked at the monitor and commented that the plane showed many feet in altitude. Roy told her that was because the airport was that many feet above sea level. From Atlanta, some of the members were going on to Florida, one to North Carolina, one to Tennessee, the rest to Louisville where they would be greeted by loved ones and friends.

Roy had the opportunity of showing his video to a group in his church. Also, the church had a TV program on which the video was shown. He combined the first mission trip with this one and was able to show it to the Buffalo Baptist Church.

CHAPTER 34

In the fall of 2008, after Roy was ready to go to teach in the adult education program, he began to have a funny feeling in his head and lay on the bed. His daughter heard the commotion and came to his room to check on him. When she began to ask questions, he could not answer in a recognizable voice or no answer at all. She called Rena where she was teaching GED in a juvenile facility to inform her of the situation. Rena told Letha to call EMS and she would meet them at the hospital.

When EMS came, one of the technicians thought it might be related to the diabetes and started to check Roy's sugar level. Because the technician's glucometer didn't work, he had to use Roy's glucometer that indicated the sugar level was in the normal range. Because the symptoms were like a stroke, EMS took him to Jewish Hospital where there is a unit for that purpose. After tests were run, nothing indicated a stroke. In the meantime his speech began to get back to normal. The attending doctor decided to keep him overnight for observation. The next day when Roy was dismissed, the doctor prescribed Coumadin as a preventive medicine for a stroke because it is a blood thinner.

A few days later, Roy remembered the morning of the incident. When he was taking his medication, he saw a pill that he questioned in his mind if it were his. A few days before, Rena had said to him that Letha had an empty pill box that held seven days of pills that he could use. He thought it was empty when he put his medicine in it. A few days later, he was looking at some of Letha's medication and saw a pill that looked like the one he thought he saw that didn't belong in his box. When he found it on the internet, one of the side effects was stroke like symptoms. Mystery solved!

About three weeks after that, Roy had been on a three hour flight and was sitting on a bench in a department store, he noticed that one of his hands was partially black where it had bled under the skin. He could not remember hitting it against anything. A man sat beside him and started a conversation. Roy showed him his hand and told him that he could not remember hitting it. The man asked, "Do you take Coumadin?"

Roy said, "Yes."

The man said that he took it and was a farmer. He said that when he was driving his tractor if it hit a bump that caused the steering wheel to jerk his hand that it turned black like that. Roy decided then that he had taken his last Coumadin since it was only a precautionary measure.

CHAPTER 35

R oy had mentioned several times to Rena that he would like to take the train from Chicago to Seattle. Shortly after that incident, she said to him, "I think that it is time for us to take the train trip to Seattle." Roy arranged the trip for June of 2009. Letha would fly from Louisville to Seattle and the three of them would fly back to Louisville.

The day before the trip, Rena and Roy flew to Chicago on Southwest Airlines. They continued on to Elgin where they visited Roy's nephews and nieces and spent the night in a motel. The next morning, they returned to Chicago and took the EL to the Chicago Union Terminal where they boarded the train to depart at 2:15 P.M. They had a roomette on the upper deck, and the meals were included in the price of the tickets. One could see some beautiful scenery along the way. The chef came through the coach to ask what each passenger wanted from the menu to eat. When meal time came, he would call the names of the passengers to come for a particular meal sitting. The car host was a great host. Each night she would turn the seat into a bed and let the upper bunk down. When the train stopped in Spokane, part of it was cut from the train and went to Portland, Oregon, and the other part went on to Seattle. While the train was approaching a tunnel through the Rocky Mountains, the train came to a stop. The conductor came on the intercom and said that there was a train ahead that had just gone through the seven and eight tenths mile long tunnel. The passenger train had to stop to let the bad air clear out of the tunnel. Then in a few minutes the train proceeded through the tunnel. When Roy asked the conductor what kept the animals out of the tunnel, he said that gates were in front of each end of the tunnel. As the train approached the tunnel the gates opened then closed after the train went through the gate.

While in Seattle, they saw the Space Needle, a native Indian play on an island, and other parks. Also there was a side trip to the top of Mt. Rainer. Wherever they went, the lines were long.

The car rental lot was next door to their hotel which was close to the airport. The night before leaving Seattle, Roy checked the auto in and took the hotel shuttle to the airport.

CHAPTER 36

In April 2011, after Rena had a mammogram, she was advised to have another one. The mammogram showed that she possibly had cancer in her right breast. The doctor performed a biopsy that confirmed she had breast cancer. When the surgeon told her when he could do the surgery, she said that she wanted to go to her granddaughter's high school graduation in another state that weekend. She did not know that this would be the last time that her granddaughter would see her alive. The surgeon set June 8, 2011, for the day of the surgery. Meanwhile, her doctor wanted her to have a stress test to see if her heart could stand the surgery. When she arrived home after the stress test, there was a message on the answering machine saying that she had an appointment with a cardiologist for a cardiac catheterization on Tuesday, June 7, 2011.

The catheterization showed that she had some serious blockages in her heart. The cardiologist told Roy and Timmy, that he didn't know if surgery for the blockages would do any good or not. The cardiologist and the breast surgeon agreed that the breast surgery should come first and deal with the heart surgery later.

Before Roy and Rena went into the hospital the day of the surgery, Roy prayed for his wife that the surgery would go well. After the surgery, the surgeon came to the waiting room and told the family that he had gotten all the cancer and that the lymph nodes looked good. That afternoon, the doctor dismissed Rena from the hospital.

After arriving home, she lay on the couch, or took it easy both that afternoon and on Thursday. Friday afternoon, she wanted Roy to walk with her in the yard to see the roses and other flowers that had been planted. After going back into the living room, she said to Roy, "I feel better now than I have felt in weeks." Roy thought that was a good sign that the healing process was going well. That night Rena slept on a couch downstairs with the door opening to the outside. About 5:15 on Saturday morning the phone beside Roy's bed rang. When he answered the phone, the voice was so garbled that he could not understand what was being said and thought it was a prank call. He put the receiver back on the cradle. Immediately, the phone rang again and the voice was clearer. Roy could then make out that it was Rena saying that she couldn't breathe and needed to go to the hospital. About the time he got downstairs to her and saw the severity of her situation, Letha came from her room. Roy told her, "Call nine one one, while I get my clothes on."

Rena then said that she wanted him to take her to the hospital. Roy replied, "You are too serious for me to take you to the hospital."

It only took EMS about five minutes to get there. In the meantime, the operator told Roy how to do CPR on Rena until the EMS arrived. After EMS came and examined her, they began to talk to see if there was anything else they could do. Roy gave them her living will and one of them said they couldn't do any more for her. As they were taking her from the room, Roy asked, "Is she still breathing?"

One of them said, "No." But the hospital records showed that her heart did not stop until after she was in the Emergency Room for a few minutes.

It seemed like more than an hour had passed after Timmy and Letha Joan, his wife, had arrived, that the doctor came to the waiting room and said that Rena had passed away. He said that a blood clot from the surgery had broken loose and went to her lungs. This was a shock to the entire family and to her friends.

Roy called Letha's ex-husband to have him inform her children that their grandmother had gone to be with Jesus. No one knew if he would bring the children for the funeral or not. He had married a Christian lady with a son and two daughters who went to his church and was a school teacher. He responded by saying that he didn't know if they could afford to come and stay in a motel. When Roy told him that they could stay at his home, they decided to come the day before the funeral and return the day after the funeral.

Following the meal after the funeral, as the group began to reminisce about the days gone by, the conversation turned into singing gospel songs that some of the group did in their church. After Rena's sister's sons told what all they did as teenagers, Roy wondered how they ever became ministers. However, one of her nephews did a great eulogy for Rena.

Roy thinks that Rena had a premonition of her death because she reminded him a few days before her death that she wanted her nephew to conduct her funeral when she died. Also, she had changed the beneficiary of an insurance policy that he didn't know she had until he examined a bank statement after her death. The Sunday before her death, she insisted that they go next door for the neighbors to witness her signing a living will.

Before Rena went home with Jesus, she told Roy that for his birthday that she was going to pay for a train ride in West Virginia. Rena died before she could fulfill the promise, so his nephew Roy went with him on the trip to Cass, West Virginia, to take the ride with a Shay steam engine. The engine pushed the train up the steep mountain. On the way down the mountain, volunteers operated the hand brakes in addition to the air brakes. There were two switchbacks on the track that made the ride interesting.

CHAPTER 37

In late August, or early September 2013, Roy's Life Group Facilitator who was a Gideon said that the Gideons ordinarily only let Gideons pass out Bibles, but they had 27,000 Bibles to hand out on a Thursday and Friday to schools, hospitals, and doctors' offices and would let others help hand them out. Roy volunteered to help distribute them. On the first day, he was able to lead three people to the Lord. The next day, the Bibles were distributed on the sidewalks near the University of Louisville. Several Gideons from different places were helping to distribute Bibles. Roy was with two other men handing the Bibles to the students as they were going to and from their classes. That morning as Roy was giving the Bibles to the students, he was able to lead seven students to Christ.

During the lunch at a nearby restaurant, one of the men who was in charge of Gideon Membership in Gideon Headquarters in Nashville encouraged Roy to become a Gideon and completed his application for him. He is able to give out Bibles and lead people to Christ which is a great blessing to him.

The most personal experience Roy had of leading someone to the Lord was his grandson, James. James was about 15 years old when his grandmother on his father's side died of Cancer. James has a twin, Joseph, and a brother who is fourteen months younger than James. Of the three, James took the death of their grandmother the hardest. After the last words were spoken at the cemetery and the last prayer was given, James was standing grieving at the foot of the casket. Being his grandfather, Roy had to comfort him somehow. Roy knew that his grandmother had trusted Christ as her Savior. Roy told James that she was in a much better place and was not in any more pain. Then, Roy told him that if he wanted to see her again that he would have to accept Christ into his life. Roy asked him if he would like to do that. James said that he did. Roy explained the plan of salvation to him. He prayed and asked Jesus to come into his heart and save him. James still tells Roy that he knows that he is saved.

CHAPTER 38

In August 2011, a volunteer, Mary, from Operation Appreciation called Roy and asked him if he would like to come to the Kentucky State Fair and help her witness from an Amazing Grace booth to fair attenders from 10:00 A.M. until 2:00 P.M. He was surprised for the number of people who accepted Christ at the fair. He volunteered with Mary and sometimes with a man who is a great witness for the Lord, who had the booth from 2:00 P.M. to 6:00 P.M., until 2013. In 2014, Mary was not able to come to the fair so the man in charge of the program had Roy to be in charge of the 10:00 A.M. until 2:00 P.M. time period. While Roy had the opportunity to lead many people to Christ, there are some that are more outstanding than others. The booth had several gospel tracts to hand out and a visual that read See three things that God cannot do with scripture verses. Each thing was behind a door that one could lift and see them: *God cannot Lie, God cannot change, and God cannot let anyone into heaven unless you are born again.*

One day, Roy noticed a man with a young child pass by the booth. In a few seconds, they returned to the booth. The man asked, "Is this an atheist thing?"

Roy replied. "No. Why do you ask that?"

The man responded, by saying that his grandson, said that it was atheist because the sign had, See Three Things God cannot do, and God can do everything. Roy let him see the three things that God cannot do, and the boy said that was true.

Roy asked the boy, "How old are you?"

He replied, "Ten"

When Roy asked him if he had been born again, he said, "No."

By this time, Roy realized that the young man had some knowledge about becoming a Christian. Roy asked him if he would like to have Christ come into his life. When he said that he would, with the grandfather's permission, Roy was able to lead the young man to Christ.

On another day, when a couple stopped by the booth, Roy was able to have a conversation with them. When the man told Roy that he was a state trooper, Roy said to him, "When you leave home in the morning, do you know if you are going to get back home at the end of the day?"

The trooper said, "No."

Roy Said, "If you don't make it back, are you one hundred percent sure that you will go to heaven?"

He replied, "No."

Roy said, "If you will let me, I can lead you in a prayer, and when we get through praying, you will know that you are one hundred percent sure that you will go to heaven."

After more conversation, Roy was able to lead both of them to Christ. They told Roy that they had wedding plans for the next summer.

A young lady who seemed to be having problems

stopped by the booth one morning. She told Roy that her mother had been shot to death a few weeks before. After further conversation, she let Roy lead her to accept Christ as a Savior.

One lady stopped by the booth and said that she knew that she was going to heaven because she prayed, went to mass, and was a good person. Then she said, "I hear people saying that they are born again, and I would like to know what they mean."

Roy's response to that was, "If you will let me, I can tell you from the Bible how you can be born again." She let Roy show her how to be born again by reading the scriptures to her, and she accepted Christ as her Savior.

In October 2015, a friend called Roy and asked him if he would like to go to the Kentucky fairgrounds to witness for the Amazing Grace Ministry at the Future Farmers of America Convention. Because of a medical condition, Roy had been restricted from driving for a period of time, so the friend would take him to the fair grounds to witness to as many people as they could. There were several other witnesses who came from other states to witness to those who came to the convention. A total of over 640 mostly young teenagers from all across The United States came to know Christ as savior. Roy had the blessing of leading about eighty people to Christ. Among them was a forty-five year old man who said that he wanted to know how to be saved. After a long conversation of his experience in a church, Roy was able to show him in the scripture how to be saved. The last person that Roy led to Christ during that convention was a young man who was having some personal issues with which Roy dealt before he left.

CHAPTER 39

As of this writing in 2017, Roy still misses Rena a great deal, but one day, as he was praying he said, "God, I thank you for the fifty-three and half years that you gave her to me. I know that with the pain that she suffered with the arthritis she would not want to come back, and she is in a much better place with You than here on Earth." That gave him some peace.

As Roy has gotten older, he has not been able to do some activities like climbing on a ladder and shoveling snow that his doctor has forbidden him to do. When snow falls, a young man who lives two doors from Roy and sometimes his brothers, clears his driveway. What a blessing! This is the same young man with his twin brother, who came to Roy's house to see if they could do anything for him when EMS was there for Rena. When they were awakened by the outside noise and saw EMS, they thought that it was Roy that needed EMS, and was surprised when they saw him outside. Their older brother, takes care of Roy's lawn and sometimes helps to clear the driveway and steps from the snow.

As of this writing in 2017, Roy goes to Ft. Knox to a Navigator's Bible Study that meets on Tuesday nights. On some Friday nights, he goes with some of the men around the barracks to give the CQs (Charge of Quarters) energy drinks and candy to help keep them stay awake all night. He gives Gideon camouflaged covered New Testaments to the soldiers who want them and has been able to lead several soldiers to the Lord through this ministry. Roy feels that God has blessed him in many ways and gives God the glory for a long life and the ability to witness for Him. He intends to keep witnessing for Christ until God calls him home or he is unable to talk.

In late November 2016, Roy had a great blessing when he was able to meet with one of his Army buddies from Germany. This was the first time that they had a chance to meet each other since October 1958 when Roy left Germany for France.

A young man whose flight had been canceled the night before was sitting next to Roy on the flight on the last leg of his flight. As the plane was descending into the airport, Roy gave him a Gideon New Testament and was able to lead him too Christ. God had a purpose for the young man's flight to be canceled.

EPILOGUE

Roy believes that every Christian should want to and be able to lead others to Christ. Jesus said in Matthew 28:19-20 K.J. Go ye therefore, unto all nations baptizing them in the name of the Father, and of the Son, and of the Holy Ghost: Teaching them to observe all things whatsoever I have commanded you and, lo, I am with you always, even unto the end of the world.

There are many ways to lead others to Christ: find one that is comfortable for yourself and use it.

If you have never accepted Christ into your life and would like to do the most important thing in your life, the following is a good way of doing that.

How to Accept Christ.

John 3:16 For God so loved the world that He gave his only begotten Son that whosoever believeth on Him should not perish, but have everlasting life.

1. Admit that you are a sinner
    Romans 3:23 For all have sinned and come short of the glory of God.

Romans 5:12 Wherefore, as by one man sin entered into the world, and death by sin; and so death passed upon all men, for that all have sinned.

It doesn't matter who we are, we have sinned because Adam sinned and we have inherited that sin nature.

Romans 6:23 For the wages of sin is death, but the gift of God is eternal life through Jesus Christ our Lord.

I John 1:10 If we say that we have not sinned, we make him a liar, and his word is not in us.

(Comment- This death is spiritual death, or eternal separation from God forever or eternity in hell; but Eternal life is spending eternity in heaven with Jesus.)

Which one do you want?

2. Be willing to repent (turn from your sin).

Luke 13:5 Jesus said, "I tell you, nay: but, except ye repent, ye shall likewise perish."

Acts 17:30 At the times of the ignorance God winked at, but now commendeth all men everywhere to repent.

3. Believe that Christ died for your sins, was buried, and rose from the dead.

John 3:16 For God so loved the world, that He gave His only begotten Son, that whosoever believeth on Him should not perish, but have everlasting life.

Romans 5:8 But God commendeth His love toward us, in that, while we were yet sinners, Christ died for us.

Romans 10:9 That if thou shalt confess with thy mouth the Lord Jesus, and shalt

Believe in thine heart that God hath raised Him from the dead, thou shalt be saved.

4. Through prayer, invite Jesus into your life to become your personal Savior.

Romans 10:10 for with the heart man believeth unto righteousness: and with the mouth confession is made unto salvation.

If you pray the following prayer and really, honestly believe and accept in faith the above scripture, God will save you and you will feel the Spirit come into your heart. Be honest with God.

Pray: Dear God, I know that I am a sinner, and I need your forgiveness. I believe that Christ died for me on the cross, and that he shed his blood for my sins on the cross. He was buried and rose again on the third day. I am willing to turn from my sins. I ask Christ to forgive me of my sins and come into my heart and life as my personal Savior. Thank you, Lord for saving me. Amen.

God doesn't lie. If you prayed in honest faith and accepted His forgiveness, you are saved and have eternal life. Romans 8: 35-39. KJV

All Scripture in this book is from the King James Version Bible.

Printed in the United States
By Bookmasters